Spiritual
ConnecTions:

Spiritual ConnecTions:

THE JOURNEY OF DISCIPLESHIP AND CHRISTIAN VALUES

BY BRIAN P. HALL

Wipf & Stock
PUBLISHERS
Eugene, Oregon

Wipf and Stock Publishers
199 W 8th Ave, Suite 3
Eugene, OR 97401

Spiritual Connections
The Journey of Discipleship and Christian Values
By Hall, Brian P.
Copyright©1991 by Hall, Brian P.
ISBN: 1-59752-701-7
Publication date 5/19/2006
Previously published by Don Bosco Press, Inc., 1991

TABLE OF CONTENTS

CHAPTER 6   113

The Disciple's Discipline

AFTERWORD   135

ENDNOTES   137

BIBLIOGRAPHY   141

APPENDIX: Value Definitions   147

FOREWORD

Discerning the authentic word of God has been a challenge for people of faith throughout the ages. In biblical times, people believe that all decisions were influenced by good or bad spirits. Therefore, when they listened to Jeremiah, Amos or any of the great prophets, they strove to determine which spirits informed the prophet's life and work. In short, they wanted to know if the prophet was a person of God or not. They wanted to know if and how God moved in the prophet's life. Likewise the prophets wanted to know if and how God moved in the people's lives. One way of determining was observance of the law of God. Behavior was important. It expressed personal commitment to God.

Jesus, like the prophets before him, understood the importance of the law, but he challenged people to move beyond simply obeying the rules and doing all the "right" things. He invited people to expand their awareness of faithfulness by living out the heart of the law, by living out what we have come to call the Gospel, or the "good news."

The Gospel of John reminds us that following the rules is no substitute for faith or a personal relationship with Jesus of Nazareth. This relationship with Jesus is expressed in the way we live our life each day. As Christians, we believe that we are called each day to follow the way of Jesus, to travel the journey of discipleship.

The purpose of this book is to help you learn practical skills for discerning God's Word in your life by exploring the spiritual connection between discipleship and values. These skills will help you understand how your values are related to God's movement in your life. By examining your values and their relationship to Scripture you will begin to know yourself better and you see more clearly ways in which you can fully follow Jesus each day. Working with your values and Scripture is a form of prayer, a way of listening to and sharing with God. By being open to the Spirit you will discover where God is moving in your life today. This is the journey of discipleship.

Benjamin Tonna
Rome
Easter 1991

Chapter 1

The Spiritual Connection: Discipleship and God's Word

*Christianity without the living Christ is inevitably
Christianity without discipleship, and
Christianity without discipleship is always
Christianity without Christ.*

Dietrich Bonhoeffer
The Cost of Discipleship

Believing is not enough. To be a follower of Christ, as Dietrich Bonhoeffer explains, means being a disciple. Perceiving and accepting the Gospel are insufficient. Our following must include perceiving, accepting and fulfilling the Gospel in our personal discipleship.

This requires a meditative stance toward life. Contemporary culture conspires against such reflection, however. We are bombarded continually with hundreds of expectations and bits of information. Dozens of claims compete for our attention. How can we keep connected to our faith when we often feel overwhelmed and uncertain? How are we to hear and sense God's direction in the midst of all the hubbub?

If we are to see the world as God sees it and live in it with God's purposes in mind, it is essential that we learn practical ways of sensing God's direction and discerning God's Word for us. Only then can we know what is best and what actions are most appropriate. This is the central task of discipleship.

Discipleship as Relationship to Christ

A critical assumption for the Christian is that God not only exists but that God cares for us and wants a loving relationship with us. God became a human being in the form of Jesus Christ to show us that we are loved so much that God became flesh like us. John says that God as "Word" became flesh, that is, became human in the person of Jesus (John 1:1, 14 and 17). For the nonbeliever listening for

God's Word would be silly, since for the nonbeliever God does not exist. The concept of discipleship is therefore for those who believe.

When I was seventeen years old I struggled with the idea of God. I was at college studying chemistry and physics and had concluded that it was logical that the universe had been set in motion by some conscious force we call God. But the real issue for me was: If God exists, could I communicate or have a relationship with him or her? I literally spent hours each week sitting alone, thinking about this and praying, "God if you really do exist, talk or say something to me."

Then, one night, I had a dream. I was standing by a barn door on a farm. The door opened and a shepherd in a long white robe came out carrying a lantern. The lantern looked like an oil lamp with a cover over it that emitted light through openings shaped like a quarter moon and the stars. The way the light shone through the lamp, it looked like the night sky.

I awoke feeling very perplexed. Then I glanced across the room and saw a copy of *A Children's Bible*[1] on the bookshelf. My father had given me the book during the war years, probably 1940. I had never opened it or read it. Without thinking I walked to the bookshelf, picked up the book and opened it. I could tell there were several glossy pages with full-page pictures on them, but they were all sealed. The pages had not been cut and separated properly. Intrigued, I got a knife from the kitchen cupboard and separated the pages. To my shock and surprise, the first picture I saw was an old classic titled "The Good Shepherd: Light of the World." It was the same shepherd I had seen in my dream. The text explained this was a picture of Jesus, the Son of God, depicted as the light of the world.

The consequence was that I became a believer, but more than that, a Christian believer, a disciple. What was important was not just the academic idea that God existed in Jesus, but that I could have a relationship with him. Once I realized this, being a Christian became an exciting proposition for me.

Jesus and Our Life as Disciples

A dimension of discipleship is learning how to live in relationship to Christ in a manner that would make him proud of us. Once the disciple understands who Christ is, namely our savior and the most important single person in human history, the issue is not only believing in him, but also how we live our faith on a day-to-day basis. The letter of James suggests that our faith has questionable value if we have nothing to show for it: "Suppose a brother or sister is in rags with not enough food for the day, and one of you says, 'Good luck to you, keep yourselves warm, and have plenty to eat,' but does nothing to supply their bodily needs, what is the good of that? So with faith, if it does not lead to action, it is in itself a lifeless thing" (James 2:15-17). Being a disciple means living out our life in a committed and specific way.

Merle Jordan has pointed out that there are so

many voices telling us what to believe and how to live our lives that it is often too difficult to sort out the trees from the forest.[2] His point is that everyone has idols or gods -- those things that absorb much of our energy and attention on a daily basis -- like the stock market, the latest fashion or even personal sickness. A key way we experience people's idol or god is not by what they say they believe, but through the manner in which they relate to other human beings. In other words, the quality of our relationships with members of our family, our friends, the people with whom we work, and even new acquaintances advertises our gods. *How we relate to people is dependent on how we see, appreciate and relate to God, not the other way around.*

Our gods are what we invest our time and energy in. They are what we think gives ultimate meaning to our lives. One young man told me recently that all he wanted out of life was to make enough money to retire by the time he was thirty. That was his god. But this god dictated the quality of the relationship with his fiancee, and how much time they spent together. She told him that she was thinking of ending the relationship because she was not a high priority in his life. From a Christian perspective his god was too small. His view of god was dictating the quality of his relationship with his fiancee.

In the dream experience that I shared with you above, I experienced God for the first time as a person who communicates to me personally and cares about me among all the other millions of persons on the planet. That was the good news. But that good news also made demands on my life, as does any serious relationship. Two people who are in love first begin to grow together by learning about each other, their family backgrounds, and their values, dreams and hopes. A relationship with God places the same demands upon us.

Learning About God through God's Word

After my dream, I had to discover how to learn about God and how to live my life in a way that reflected God's plans and possibilities for me. My journey of discovery and learning began shortly after my dream. It began in my house -- in the attic, which had not been cleared out for years. I had told my mother about my dream, and she informed me that several aunts, since deceased, had been religious. They had left some of their books with her, and the books were in the attic.

I found five or six old books dating back to about 1890. I began reading the inscriptions in the front of them and then some of the material inside one of the books. Later I came to understand that what I was reading was the Bible. In fact, I was reading the Gospel of John. I had never read a Bible before. Without thinking I began to read parts of the Book of Revelation which sounded a little like science fiction at first, with angels and archangels and battles in heaven. I also remember reading the Beatitudes from Matthew (5:1-12). "Blessed are those who show mercy" and "Blessed are the peacemakers" made a lot of sense to me as a young man trying to understand life. I was very taken by what I was reading, thrilled in fact. I started going back to the attic every day.

What was happening to me as I read, and later as I discussed what I had read with a local minister, was that my personal view of God was different from what I was experiencing through the Scriptures. In fact, the Scripture was challenging me to be different. What I now understand is that my relationship with God was changing the way I viewed and thought about people, my life, and what I wanted to do with it. I was learning that the way the disciple grows in relationship with God, with Jesus of Nazareth, is through reading Scripture and listening to what God has to say through the Word.

Spiritual Connection: God and God's Word

Critical to spirituality is having a minimum understanding of what constitutes reality: what the world is about, how it functions and how God fits into this reality. This is at the heart of what we mean by "spiritual connections." Each epoch of human history -- since the beginning of human language -- has expanded our view of reality and the world we live in. What we know now through religion and the sciences such as astronomy and physics is only a partial picture of reality, but it is much expanded from what we knew several hundred years ago.

We cannot know God as we can know a human being. We cannot see and touch God like we can see and touch a lover, a parent or a child we gave birth to. God is mysterious, awesome and totally beyond our comprehension. God is the creator of all the universe and is infinitely wise, wiser than any person. But unlike other religions, Christianity is beautifully blessed with the gift of Christ. God became human to help us bridge this gigantic gap of unknowing -- giving us the promise of care and intimacy as well as the ability to discover the joy, pain and expectations of what it means to be a disciple. We cannot comprehend God, but we can know some things about God and what the Creator expects of us through Jesus.

Creation and God's Word

In the Gospel of John, we read, "In the beginning was the Word, and Word was with God, and the Word was God. He was in the beginning with God. All things came into being through him, and without him not one thing came into being. What has come into being through him is life, and the life was the light of all people" (John 1: 1-4).

When we compare the original Greek text of the first verse of John -- "In the beginning was the Word" -- with the Greek version of the first of Genesis 1:1, we find the text is exactly the same but with one word change. In Genesis we read, "In the beginning was God." John substitutes the "Word" for "God" and writes, "In the beginning was the Word." Why does John use the expression "Word" as a way of talking about God? What is he saying about the nature of God that is important to us as disciples?

John and the authors of Genesis understood that there is a direct connection between language -- the "Word" or words of God -- and creative, life-giving action. The book of Genesis begins by talking about how God created through the spoken Word: "In the beginning of creation, when God made heaven and the earth, the earth was a formless void, and darkness covered the face of the deep, while a wind from God swept over the face of the waters. Then God said, 'Let there be light,' and there was light; and God saw that the light was good" (Gen. 1:1-4). What we see here is that the power of God's spoken Word creates order out of chaos; God's Word creates life itself. This theme is repeated throughout Genesis. In the following examples, note the relationship between God's spoken Words and the creation that results from those words:

"And God said, 'Let the waters under the sky be gathered together into one place, and let the dry land appear.' And it was so" (Gen. 1:9). "Then God said, 'Let the earth put forth vegetation: plant yielding seeds, and fruit trees of every kind on earth that bear with the seed in it,' and it was so" (Gen. 1:11). "And God said, 'Let the waters bring forth swarms of living creatures, and let birds fly above the earth across the dome of the sky.' And so God created the great sea monsters and every living creature that moves, of every kind, and every winged bird of every kind. And God saw that it was good" (Gen. 1:20-21).

Here we encounter great beauty and mystery,

for in each verse it is what God said, or God's Word, that is the occasion for the creation. In the Gospel of John the evangelist refers to God and Jesus as this Word. For the authors of Genesis and John, the "Word" is not only synonymous with God but also expresses the understanding that language and God are connected.

This connection between God and language takes on a personal significance and meaning when we realize that the way we relate to other people reflects the way we see and understand God. In a very concrete way, our language -- the way we speak to and with others -- can create life or cause great hurt. We can create life in those to whom we speak, just as God created life itself through the spoken words of Genesis 1. Words of blame and accusation can bring great hurt to our loved ones, whereas a gentle "I love you" or "I am so proud of you" can transform a person's day and sometimes his or her life. This is why John writes: "What has come into being through him is life, and the life was the light of all people" (John 1:1-4).

When we speak a word of love to someone, God's Word within us is activated and the person can experience God's love through us in that moment. To understand how and why this happens, we must look at Genesis and what I call the *Genesis Effect*.

The Genesis Effect and God's Word

To say that God's Word is within us is a big jump from only seeing God as the creator of the universe around us. This God, or Word of God within, is also anticipated in Genesis (1: 26-27), "Then God said, 'Let us make humankind in our image, according to our likeness, and let them have dominion over the fish of the sea, and over the birds of the air, and over the cattle, and over all the wild animals, and over every creeping thing that creeps upon the earth.' And so God created humankind in his image, in the image of God he created them male and female he created them."

"Let us make humankind in our image" implies that a design for what was human existed in God's mind before the human was created through God's Word. The Hebrew term that we translate as "image" usually denotes a concrete physical likeness, but it also refers to the spiritual attributes symbolized by the physical body. The word "image" for the writer is also connected with the previous verse stating that humankind will have dominion over the creation. Thus "image" carries with it a corporeal sense of the erect human that rules creation and the inner spiritual dimension of the being that has conscious moral dignity. Thus "image" of humankind is really manifest in its fullest potential in the person of Jesus.

That we are made in the image of God means not only that we were created by God's Word, as was all creation, but it means also that an image of humankind -- after which we were patterned -- existed in God's mind prior to our creation. God's Words (language) convey the power that creates. Man and woman become reality by the spoken

Word of God the Creator.

That image preceded God's spoken Words is an incredible thought. We now know through studies of the brain that we human beings create images, or pictures if you will, of everything we do before we actually do it.[3] The idea of an image existing before something becomes real may sound strange to us, yet we often think this way ourselves. For example, when we plan to go to the beach on vacation, we usually fantasize about it and imagine what it will be like before we go. When we think about it, we are actually picturing or imagining it, creating an "image" of it. We imagine we are relaxing on the beach, listening to the waves lapping on the warm sand. We imagine the blue of the ocean and the inviting aroma wafting toward us from the hot dog stand nearby. Our image of the beach exists before it becomes "real" in our lives, before we get there on vacation. We do this "imaging" or "imagining" with everything that we do. When we decorate our homes, we first imagine what it will look like if we put the couch here or by the window, or if we paint the living room beige instead of blue.

We are children of God, created in God's own image, and just as we were created in God's image, we also use images as we "create" our lives each day. Our internal images of who we are, what we want to do, how we want to handle our lives each day can be expressed in language, in words. For example, when we tell someone about our hopes for a better situation at work -- our "image" of a healthier work environment -- we communicate our image through language. Basically we think and imagine through our dreams and plans; language helps make our inner images become real.

The concept of "Word" as God's speech that creates and gives life -- a word that is preceded by an image of that which is created such as, humankind -- points to the reality of the interior dimension of our lives. What do our inner images have to do with our faith? What do they have to do with discipleship? Our inner image of God precedes and directs our daily decisions and the quality of our human relationships.

Our inner world of images and dreams is related to the outer world of people, places and things. I call this spiritual connectedness of our inner and outer lives, and the creative consequences of this connectedness the *Genesis Effect*. The Genesis Effect is the process whereby our internal images act upon and transform the world we live in. For example, if I have an inner image of how family conflicts should be resolved, that image will influence how I deal with an argument between the kids over who gets to watch what on TV, or when homework should be done in relation to play time.

Values are a part of this process too. They are priorities upon which we act, and they are also words we use in the language.[4] Values mediate images and transform them into our everyday behavior -- the way we live as disciples of Christ.

Therefore our inner image of who God is precedes and directs the way we behave on a day-to-day basis. The quality of our relationships and our discipleship is a consequence of how we see God.

We all live with our feet in two worlds at the same time: the external world of societies, institutions, family and friends, and the internal world of fantasy, images and the unconscious. Naturally God is Lord of both these worlds. When God became human in the person of Jesus, humanity was introduced to this inner dimension. Jesus spoke the words that transformed those first disciples into people who lived their lives energized by the values and concerns that God wishes for all of us. John expresses this in Jesus' prayer, "I have made your name known to those whom you gave me from the world. They were yours and you gave them to me, and they have kept your word. Now they know that everything you have given me is from you; for the words that you gave to me I have given to them, and they have received them and know in truth that I came from you; and they have believed that you sent me" (John 17: 6-8).

This mysterious passage shows how God as Word, in the spoken Word of Jesus, transforms the disciples' experience of God. That experience of Word in the life of the disciples changed the way they related to one another and the way they related to the early Christian community -- they initiated the church in history.

But we have no one to talk directly to us as Jesus did to his disciples! So how do we get this same life-giving experience of the Word? We get it from reading the Bible, as I did in the attic in my home. This is why Jesus as Word continues and is such a gift to anyone who wants to listen and become a disciple.

Conclusion: The Power of the Word

We've talked about the power of the spoken Word -- both God's and our own. We have looked at the relationship between our inner images and the way we act in the world, and how the spoken Word (language) mediates, or makes a connection, between our inner and outer worlds. We also saw that God's spoken Word created the world, and we saw that Christ's spoken Word transformed the disciples.

For John the Word and Jesus are inextricably tied together "And the Word became flesh, and lived among us and we have seen his glory, the glory as of a father's only Son, full of grace and truth" (John 1:14). Jesus manifests the Word. The word is no longer something abstract and distant; in Jesus the Word is enfleshed, "incarnated" in our lives. Jesus is a living part of our daily lives. The Word comes from God and is God.

We know the Word of God has power in our lives, but we often forget that our words have power too. The Word that we know as Jesus is related to the ordinary words that each of us speaks and listens to each day, because words are one way we live out our faith. Just as the Word is powerful, so are "Words." They help us communicate with and understand one another. Words also help us to bring our hopes and our dreams, our thoughts and our ideas into concrete existence.

We experience and exercise the power of words each day. When we speak to our family or friends, coworkers or strangers, our words can be creative or destructive, life-affirming or life-denying. The ancients knew that language is powerful. Jesus' Word changes water into wine, heals the blind, and turns ordinary people into apostles and disciples. This is what God's Word can do for us too.

Why is it that the words someone speaks can make us laugh or cry? What is it in language that made the Words of Jesus so powerful to those first century hearers? What did he touch in so many people? When Jesus healed the blind man, fed the five thousand and called each of the disciples, he responded to critical human needs. What was it in him that made this dynamic connection with so many who heard him? His values connected him with the hearer. Values such as [Self]Worth, Care, Human Dignity and Justice appear throughout the Gospels. *Values energized Jesus of Nazareth, and values energize and transform us into true disciples.*

To be a disciple of Jesus is to own and act on the values that energized him. The New Testament letter of James tells us that simply to say we believe in Jesus is not enough. We must also strive to be as loving as Jesus was. Faith means believing in Jesus as our savior, getting to know his Word in Scripture and making it our work in our daily living. We do this by valuing what Jesus valued.

During the last twenty-five years I have spent most of my time studying values in human and spiritual development and how values relate to what we have been discussing: "Word." I am now convinced that our values mediate between our inner world of images and the external observable world of our everyday lives through the spoken language. Our values are a way of understanding both our inner life and our external behavior, understanding where we are in our journey of discipleship. Through our values we can discover precisely how and what God's Word is saying to us.

Chapter 2

Values, Signs And God's Word

*By the virtues of Christ we mean the excellence of
character which on the one hand he exemplifies in
his own life, and which on the other he
communicates to his followers.*

Richard Niebuhr
Christ and Culture

The good news of the Gospel is that God became a human being in the form of Jesus of Nazareth to convey the reality that each of us is of infinite value to God. To understand this is to be a disciple. An important dimension of this is to live out our lives based on that belief. The bottom line of such a belief is the idea that God has declared that each of us is unique and has special qualities and, as such, has particular gifts to offer to the world.

Language distinguishes humans from the lower animals. It is language that allows our innermost thoughts to be shared with others and expands our world a hundredfold every time we enter into a loving relationship with another person. The very essence of discipleship is communication, we experience and grow through God's Word as it speaks to us through the spirit within each of us, as it speaks to us through Scripture and as it speaks to us through the mystery of the incarnation as we talk lovingly with each other.

Not only does God care for us and value us and our humanity, but God also calls each of us to discipleship to help bring about a new world order. In other words, from God's point of view what is important is that disciples be the kind of people that will make the kingdom come alive on earth. In order for this to happen, disciples must have the kinds of qualities that Jesus talks about in the Gospels. The apostle Paul summarizes these qualities, behaviors and expectations in his first letter to the Corinthians, "And now faith, hope and love abide, these three; and the greatest of these is love." (Cor. 13:13). These qualities we call values.

I believe values are critical to the growth and transformation of both people and institutions, and that values are signs of God's action in our lives. *Values are priorities by which we choose to live our lives. They are designated by special "code" words in our spoken and written language, paralleled in the experience of God's revelation through Scripture, experienced through our feelings and imagination, and acted on repeatedly and consistently.*

Values, then, are priorities that we feel are important to us and that can serve as signs of God in our lives. Christians follow certain values that are intrinsic to their faith. These values are what Niebuhr calls "the virtues of Christ." They are basic to discipleship and to what each of us can become as disciples. In this chapter, we will look at how our values can be signs of God's movement in our lives, and how those values are related to God's Word. Together these will help us understand more clearly what it means to be a disciple.

An Experience of the Word

At the break of day on Christmas morning in 1967, I walked toward the small house of Dona Teresa in Barrio Cuba, on the outskirts of San Jose, Costa Rica. Two drunks lying in a doorway cursed and threatened me as I came in sight of her house, a wooden shack clustered with several others on a steep slope. At the bottom of the slope was the river where everyone washed, drank, and cooked.

Dona Teresa's house served both as the meeting place for the barrio congregation of which I was pastor and as the community television room. A few moments after I arrived, I stood behind the television set, draped now with a clean white cloth and topped with a Bible opened to John's Gospel. For some time we had been reflecting with difficulty on the idea of the "Word made flesh" in Jesus. With that in mind, I asked, "What is the *problema* -- the problem -- that we face together in Barrio Cuba?"

The barrio consisted of about 70,000 people, most of whom did not make enough money to feed their families each week. Prostitution as a way of surviving flourished. Alcoholism and other addictions were rampant. The house where we met was infested with cockroaches. Rats occasionally darted across the floor in front of the children or behind the kitchen sink. Most of the parents in that room had as many as fifteen children -- of whom only a few had survived. The children in any given family often had several different fathers.

For months I had been with these people asking the same question: What is the real problem that we face? Pastoral training had led me to this barrio. My task was simply to listen to the people and spot emotionally laden words. My mentors had told me that emotionally laden words would be like road signs pointing to the real problems in the barrio.[1] People continually talked about the *problema*. Therefore at a very simple level I had chosen that word "problema." Whenever people mentioned it I simply asked them -- children, fathers, mothers -- what they felt the real problem to be. Many viewed prostitution as the worst problem. Girls as young as ten or eleven often became prostitutes. But not everyone was sure that this was "The Problem."

That Christmas morning when I asked, "What is the problem we face?" A woman responded. Her husband had been missing for two weeks and she had come to church with three of her children. Slowly she said, "When I make love with a man, even when it is not right some times, then at least in the middle of this dirt and these problems I feel like a human being, just for a little bit." Silence reigned. Then someone spoke up and asked, "What does God have to say about that?"

It is difficult, even after twenty years, to comprehend all that happened at that meeting. Several others shared the same thought, and we talked about how God became human to show us how deeply God loves us and how lovable we are. The *problema*, I concluded, was [Self]Worth, a value missing in their lives but a gift that God brought them on that Christmas Day. So valuable was that gift to the community that in the following months the people organized a child day care center in the barrio. This allowed women to work and provide for their families along with their husbands. It did not eliminate prostitution in the barrio but it did save some children from its horror and brought forgiveness and life to others.

Discernment: Values as Signs of God's Action

That courageous woman shared the depths of herself, and the people around her confirmed that she was loved and forgiven. This experience can be summarized by one word that has to do with being human: [Self]Worth. The value of [Self]Worth (number 125 in the comprehensive list in the Appendix) is defined as "The knowledge that when those one respects and esteems really know him/her, they will affirm that he/she is also worthy of that respect."

Several passages in Scripture refer to this value. The Gospel of John (3: 16) expresses this value -- God loves and esteems us so much that Jesus became human in order to save us. [Self]Worth in Christian terms means accepting the gift of the incarnation in Jesus Christ as the sign that we are truly known and esteemed by God.

The group in the barrio experienced new life as a result of discovering the value of [Self]Worth. Meetings now seemed charged with energy. Whenever I think of the value "[Self]Worth," it becomes linked with a series of images and experiences I had with those people over the months we spent together. I also think of the Scripture passages that make such an event a God event and not just a human one. What we had discovered was a value critical in the lives of those people.

Values occupied my research for the next twenty years. During that time I discovered 125 value words in the written and spoken language that expand the awareness and meaning of people's lives.[2]

Each of the values represents a priority human experience. Each also represents behaviors that influence our daily actions when we consider the value to be important. For Christians it is equally important that each of the values has a parallel experience in Scripture. As such, we see [Self] Worth as the value in which we experience the incarnation of God's love in our own lives.

Values are an enormous source of information about our nature as human beings and our relationship to God. In fact, *values are signs of God's action in our lives, priorities which direct our behavior.* The ability to judge whether or not a person's behavior is from God is a very ancient spiritual discipline referred to as the "discernment of spirits."

In Old Testament times observable behavior (adherence to the law) was considered crucial to discerning whether or not God was moving in people's lives. Jesus took this one step farther by challenging people to move beyond simple obedience and inviting them to live out the heart of the law, which we have now come to call the "good news" or Gospel. God's action can be seen in people's lives as they embrace and live out the good news.

Looking for signs of God's action is not limited to observing the behavior of individuals but includes watching institutions as well. Consider Paul's letter to the Galatians. Paul is concerned about infighting in a local congregation. First, he lists all the negative behaviors the congregation should avoid, such as idolatry, drunkenness and sorcery (5:19-21). Next, he instructs the leadership in the signs to look for that show movement beyond mere rules to the heart of what Gospel living is about: "By contrast, the fruit of the Spirit is love, joy, peace, patience, kindness, generosity, faithfulness, gentleness and self control. If we live by the Spirit let us also be guided by the Spirit" (5:22-23, 25).

These signs were an early list of Christian values. They were a way of determining whether or not a group of people were living Gospel values. The values listed in the appendix are human values -- accessible to everyone. A question arises that we need to address before going any further. What is the relationship between Christian (Gospel) values and human values?

Values or Virtues?

Values are an inherent and essential aspect of what it means to be human. They are at the core of our language and are the very core of human motivation and transformation. Nearly 2500 years ago, Aristotle, one of the first to raise the values issue, asked: What does it mean to be an excellent human being? He concluded that it meant being a person who had virtue. For Aristotle, virtues were those human qualities which make a person good. He included wisdom, understanding, temperance and prudence. The virtues were hierarchical. That is, some, such as wisdom, were thought to be superior to others.

In the 1960s, the question of values emerged as a central theme in U.S. public life. It was a period of great turmoil. National heroes who epitomized our values, such as John and Robert Kennedy and Martin Luther King, Jr. were assassinated. The country was embroiled in a war to which it was not committed. Schools faced dramatic increases in drug experimentation by students. Issues of racial and sexual equality and human rights became critical concerns.

During this time interest in values emerged in the fields of psychology and education. In 1965, Louis Rath, Merrill Harmin and Sidney Simon authored a book titled *Values and Teaching* which ushered in a phenomenon known as the "values clarification movement." In the book the authors defined values as those elements that show how a person has decided to use his or her life.[3] They were more interested in the process of valuing than in the content of values in morally healthy people. Consequently, many churches condemned values clarification because it lacked a moral or Christian dimension.

Historically values and virtues have always been connected. Every culture and religion has its own unique ethical list of those human attributes that make up the virtuous person. These ethical lists are lists of values. Virtues pertain to certain values that a culture or religion feels should take a priority in a person's life for that person to be considered excellent or good.

Christ models for Christians priority values or virtues. Christianity's list of virtues has traditionally been the one written by Paul, "And now faith, hope and love abide, these three; and the greatest of these is love" (1 Cor. 12-13).

These values were seen as virtues, that is, values higher in priority than other values. Additionally, Paul sees love as the highest priority of all. Virtues are a hierarchy of values. Paul's letter gives us guidance about what values we need and in what order they should be prioritized to be an excellent Christian person.

Christian or Gospel Values

As we have seen above, values such as faith, hope and love are always present with other values. They always form hierarchies. When we discussed the experience of the congregation in Barrio Cuba, we concentrated on their experience of the love of God through the value of [Self]Worth. In reality this value was in relationship to other values that the people of the barrio held.

In addition to the discovery of [Self]Worth, which was not originally even in their awareness, the members of the congregation in Barrio Cuba were coping with the survival of their families. Their primary values were minimal: Family/Belonging, [Self]Preservation, Community/Support and [Self]Worth. (See Appendix.) Before and after the experience we might imagine they were prioritized as follows:

Before the Experience	After the Experience
[Self]Preservation	[Self]Worth
Family/Belonging	Family/Belonging

| (Community/Support) | Community/Support |
| ([Self]Worth) | [Self]Preservation |

In my early experience with the people in the barrio [Self]Preservation absorbed all the energy of most of the families. The situation was so extreme that the primary function of the Family was to provide what was necessary for survival, even if it meant, in some extreme cases, prostituting the children. As such, the values of Community/Support and [Self]Worth were practically nonexistent. (Note they are in parentheses in the list.) The world was a very alien and hostile place for these people.

In the second column, which represents the events at the meeting on Christmas morning, we see a major shift in the value priorities. The value of [Self]Worth emerges and is enhanced by a supportive and nurturing community. This, in turn, leads to a different idea of what a family is. [Self] Preservation is now prioritized after Family/Belonging. This new priority led the group to initiate, in the months to come, a family orientation clinic that provided family planning information, child development education and day care opportunities for families of mothers who wished to work. What happened that Christmas morning to generate so much creative energy? We can identify the following:

- Two new values -- [Self]Worth and Community/Support -- emerged and were recognized by the people.
- Value priorities changed.

- The change in value priorities altered perceptions of what was understood by Family. The understanding of Family changed from something necessary for survival to something that nurtures and loves children and provides some belonging and comfort.

In other words, when the priorities changed, the quality of each person's values changed. Putting it another way, their consciousness of themselves as individuals and the people around them changed. This in turn radically changed their daily behavior.

There is also an important group dimension to this experience. When we look up the Scripture passages related to these values, we see that Community/Support relates to the Christian understanding of the Body of Christ, which emphasizes the gifts and relatedness of each of us to the person of Christ. Originally the barrio congregation was a small group of independent persons. After the Christmas morning experience, they became a nurturing community of listeners with a common experience of Christ's love. In fact, I believe it was precisely this communal dimension, the experience of Christ's Body, that permitted the group to transcend itself and grow productively. It became clear that, one person's values can influence others. Originally family life, which is a form of institutional life, was necessary for survival. In Barrio Cuba, however, after the Christmas morning experience the family expanded beyond survival and became a place where God's Word could permeate and be a sustaining power for the children and their parents.

So we see that the value of [Self]Worth was related to all the other value priorities that the people had. Since the experience took place within the context of the Christian community, the entire group was transformed. As a community the people oriented their values toward enhancing life for the children. The resulting value priorities were a sign of God's action in that community. The experience was life-giving for the community. In Christian terms it was a resurrection experience -- an experience when people are reborn and given life in a way they had not experienced it before.

We have been looking at values in general. Now we are ready to look at a definition of Christian values, or what some call Gospel values, as a matter of further clarification. *Christian or Gospel values are priorities that determine how we live our lives. They are designated by special "code" words in the spoken and written language; paralleled in the experience of God's revelation through Scripture; experienced through our feelings and imagination; acted on repeatedly and consistently; and are life-giving (resurrection) to us and the community of believers at large.*

Conclusion: The Genesis Effect Revisited

We have discussed values as an inherent part of language. They are priorities upon which we act and they are also words we use. Values mediate our images and transform them into our everyday behavior -- the way we live as disciples of Christ. The diagram below illustrates:

GENESIS 1

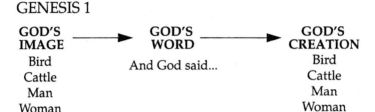

GOD'S IMAGE	GOD'S WORD	GOD'S CREATION
Bird	And God said...	Bird
Cattle		Cattle
Man		Man
Woman		Woman

In the book of Genesis, God's Word is preceded by an image of the creation. When God speaks, "Let the waters bring forth swarms of living creatures, and let birds fly above the earth across the dome of the sky" (Gen. 1: 20-21), the creation gives forth birds. In the same way, humankind is imaged, God speaks, and men and women are created. We see the same parallel in human communication, which after all, is also a product of God's Word.

INTERNAL IMAGE	LANGUAGE & VALUES	EXTERNAL REALITY
Wife	Care/Nuture	Love poem
Grassy plain	Awe of Nature	Painting
Winning tennis	Competition	Playing tennis
Student	Education	Taking exams

We have internal images that precede whatever it is that we are doing. A man wants to tell his wife that he loves her and writes a love poem about how he cares for her. He expresses this through language, by the written word, which takes the internal images and feelings of love and care and enables him to translate his inner thoughts into a poem. An artist has an image of a grassy green plain filled with flowers. The value of Wonder/Nature enables the artist to express this creatively as a painting that everyone can see. A student wanting to be a professor is motivated by the value of Education to take courses and study for exams. And finally the value of Competition links the internal image of winning at tennis with the external reality of being a tennis player.

These examples help us to see the relationship between our internal images, our language and values, and external reality. But what is the relationship between God's Word, human values and Gospel values? The following diagram will help us to make this connection.

GENESIS 2

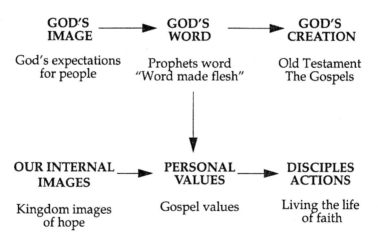

GOD'S IMAGE ——→ GOD'S WORD ——→ GOD'S CREATION

God's expectations for people   Prophets word "Word made flesh"   Old Testament The Gospels

OUR INTERNAL IMAGES ——→ PERSONAL VALUES ——→ DISCIPLES ACTIONS

Kingdom images of hope   Gospel values   Living the life of faith

This diagram represents present reality as we disciples struggle to know the Lord at this time. God is unknowable except where God has been made known to us through the prophets and through Jesus. Obviously we cannot know what

God imagined, but we do know what God expected of the chosen people through the history of the covenant. The ten commandments are the central covenant of the Old Testament setting out God's minimal expectations for human behavior. This is represented in the left column "God's expectations for people."

This expectation (God's image) is revealed to us through God's words (middle column) spoken by the prophets in the Old Testament (third column). Similarly Jesus of Nazareth was revealed to the first disciples and apostles as God's "Word made flesh." This in turn we experience by the reading of the Gospels.

What is essential and exciting is that the Word made flesh in Jesus and experienced in Scripture is also present to us through our interior life, our inner world. The connecting point is our values, when they are Gospel values. We activate those values when we are inspired with images of the kingdom -- a new order in line with the vision of Jesus. Those values then give us life, as they gave life to the people in Barrio Cuba. We are energized by the same values that energized Jesus.

When he left the disciples, Jesus promised to send another to speak in his name who would be with them whenever they spoke the word of truth. "When the Advocate comes whom I will send to you from the Father, the Spirit of truth who comes from the Father, he will testify on my behalf. You also are to testify because you have been with me from the beginning" (John 15: 26-27).

The Spirit of Christ, as advocate or counselor within us, is activated when we speak as disciples in his name. The Gospel of John reminds us that this relationship with Jesus is expressed in the way we live our lives each day. As Christians, we believe that we are called each day to follow the way of Jesus, to travel the journey of discipleship.

A part of discipleship is understanding how we experience and express our faith in and through our values, and exploring ways in which those values can help us grow in our relationship with God. Our day-to-day choices reflect our values in the way we live. These values, therefore, reflect our faith and express how we currently live out the Gospel life of discipleship.

One way to understand and fully live out this daily discipleship is to turn inward and reflect on our values as signs of God's action in our lives. A way to begin this reflection is to review the values in the appendix and choose six that are your highest priorities. Reflect on them and the Scripture listed with them.[4]

To be a disciple is to be a learner and a follower. Disciple comes from the Latin word *discipulus* which means "pupil." Christian discipleship, then, is the practice of learning from and following Jesus. As disciples we seek to grow in our relationships with God, Jesus Christ and the Holy Spirit -- the Creator, Redeemer and Sanctifier. Just as Jesus became human and entered fully into life, God enters our lives each day. Discipleship means discovering, following and acting on the signs for faithful living that God gives us each day. A part of this is understanding our values as Gospel values.

Chapter 3

Faith, Hope and Love: Gospel Values as Gifts

Now there are varieties of gifts, but the same Spirit; and there are varieties of services, but the same Lord; and there are varieties of activities, but it is the same God who activates them all of them in everyone. To each is given the manifestation of the Spirit for the common good.

1 Corinthians 12:4-8

Values as Gifts of the Spirit

The Spirit gives each of us different gifts. These gifts enable us to live our lives in the unique way God calls us. But we don't always recognize the gifts we have been given. Therefore a part of our faith journey -- our journey of discipleship -- is discerning our gifts and learning to use them as expressions of our faith each day.

Our values represent and help reveal the multitude of gifts the Spirit has given us. Looking at our values can help us discover, understand and begin to use our spiritual gifts. Our value priorities make each of us unique and different from others with whom we work and play. This is because each of the values we have requires its own skills. If an important value for me is Education, then I have to become learned or educated. That is, I have to learn the skills related to this important value.

Paul writes eloquently of the variety of spiritual gifts: "To one is given through the Spirit the utterance of wisdom, and to another the utterance of knowledge according to the same Spirit, to another faith by the same Spirit, to another gifts of healing by the one Spirit, to another the working of miracles, to another prophecy; to another discernment of spirits, to another various kinds of tongues, to another the interpretation of tongues. All these are activated by one and the same Spirit, who allots to each one individually just as the Spirit chooses" (1 Cor 12: 8-11).

Just as all parts are essential to the physical body (1 Cor 12:12), we -- with all our different gifts and values -- are essential parts of the Body of Christ. This is what Paul means when he writes "To each is given the manifestation of the Spirit for the common good" (1 Cor 12:7). But there is another very important element in all this which helps distinguish between human values and Gospel values. That element is the concept of "Gifts." Gifts are the ways in which we act upon our values for the benefit of the community -- the ways in which we show love to one another. Gifts transform human values into Gospel values.

Yet at each and every point in our development, we can either grow spiritually or run the risk of regressing. Understanding this and how we develop our Gospel values is what this chapter is about.

Faith, Hope and Love

The three values of Faith, Hope and Love have formed the heart of virtuous discipleship for centuries. It is important for us to understand that these three values are intricately connected. We see this connection vividly in the life of Jesus.

Many writers and biblical scholars point out that Jesus was driven by Hope -- his dream for a better world -- for the establishment of God's Kingdom on earth.[1] He chose twelve disciples to symbolize the new Israel and the new twelve tribes -- the catalyst for a better world. Everything he did in his short life was directed to his dream, and today the churches are a living continuation of Christ's Hope.

The manner in which he lived out that Hope on a day-to-day basis reveals the Faith of Jesus. His constant risk-taking -- preaching this Hope against overwhelming hostility -- resulted in his death on the cross. Jesus had Faith in the future and in God's love. He acted upon Hope and Faith out of Love -- a desire to benefit the community. Love is the way Jesus acted upon his Hope and Faith in order to bring about the Kingdom of God. Jesus lived out his Faith and Hope through Love. The following diagram illustrates this point.

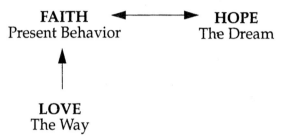

FAITH ◄———► **HOPE**
Present Behavior   The Dream

▲

LOVE
The Way

The way in which values are connected is at the heart of what we mean by Gospel values. Faith and Hope, in the diagram above, are long term goals. Christ's long-term commitment was to live out a long-term vision of the future of humankind (Hope) on a day-by-day basis (Faith), by means of being loving in the present (Love). Love was the gift that Jesus used for the benefit of the community. He expressed this love by caring for his disciples, by healing the sick and by dying for all of us. His Faith was evident in his willingness to die; his Hope was realized in the resurrection. Both Faith and Hope were activated by Love, transforming the otherwise human values into Gospel values.

This same connection of Gospel values is evident in our lives as disciples. Here is one example from my life. At lunch one day my friend Rita informed me that she had cancer and was going to die. Naturally I was shocked, and I asked her how she had come to this conclusion. It seemed that she had been having problems with her stomach for several years, and during a recent medical exam the doctor had detected a lump in her upper intestine. The next morning she was scheduled for a tissue biopsy.

"Why do you feel you have cancer if you are only going in for exploratory surgery?" I asked. Rita responded, "I just know, that's all!" Both her sister and mother had died of cancer, and she was obviously very afraid that it was also going to happen to her. When I offered to accompany her so that she would not have to be alone in the morning, Rita became very angry.

I disregarded her angry response and appeared at the doctor's office to sit with her before she went into surgery. Rita said nothing. When the nurse called her name, I wished her luck and said, "I'll go now and come back in a couple of hours when this is over." Anxiously she spoke for the first time, "Please don't go. Will you stay until I come out?"

I agreed and waited until the surgery was over. As we left the office over two hours later, the nurse cautioned Rita, "Try not to worry. We will have the results in two days."

Rita asked me to go and have coffee with her in a nearby twenty-four-hour diner. We sat, talked, drank coffee -- and ate occasionally -- for nearly two days! She was terrified to hear the test results. Finally lacking sleep, missing work and neglecting a thousand things at home, I was becoming very resentful, though I tried hard not to show it. About three o'clock on the second day I suggested, "Why don't I call the doctor's office for you and ask the nurse if the results are in yet?" Rita nodded. When I called the nurse reported there was no cancer.

Later when we discussed the whole experience, I was laughing about how "uptight" I was at the end of the two days. Rita looked at me and said, "That didn't matter. You were loving me anyway! I was so scared I needed you to hope for me."

Her response surprised me. I was doing what a lot of Christians do everyday for people they love. I had been irritated, but I loved her the best I could with my limitations. I was there because of the hope -- not simply the hope that she would not have cancer, but that I would be with her to discover God's will in her life no matter what the outcome. My faith kept me at her side. Love enabled me to be present for her, transforming the human values of faith and hope into Gospel values.

When all our other values share the same priorities -- faith, hope and love -- that energized Jesus of Nazareth, they become Gospel values.

Faith, Hope, Love: The Foundation of All Christian Values

Faith and Hope are the long-term goals of all who call ourselves disciples. Our vision, like Christ's, is for the kingdom to become a reality on earth. Our faith calls us to live that out on a day-to-day basis. C. H. Dodd, in his commentary on faith in Paul's letters, writes, "....We may say that for Paul faith is that attitude in which, acknowledging our complete insufficiency for any of the high ends of life, we rely utterly on the sufficiency of God."[2] Dodd goes on to say, "There is no ultimate value in any religious attitude, unless it is directed towards the one and only God. 'God is trustworthy' (1 Cor.1:9; 10:13; 1 Thess. 5:24) is the fundamental principle to which our faith is the response."[3]

Love holds all this together. As the diagram of the interaction of Faith, Hope and Love illustrates, Faith and Hope are meaningless without Love. Paul says, "For now we see in a mirror, dimly, but then we will see face to face. Now I know only in part; then I will know fully, even as I have been fully known, And now faith, hope and love abide, these three; and the greatest of these is love" (1 Cor. 13:12-13).

Most of the 125 values can be an expression of Love when they are connected with the other value priorities that energized Jesus, namely Faith and Hope, transforming them into Gospel values. Faith and Hope are the spiritual connections, generated or activated by Love. Each of us loves unique to our values, our gifts and the needs of the situation.

Let us look at some examples of loving expressed by various values with their applicable
Scripture references:

10. **Care/Nurture:** To be physically and emotionally supported by family and friends
throughout one's life and to value doing the
same for others. The concept is that we
should care for ourselves and others as God
cares for us.

Matt. 6: 24-34; Gal. 5: 13-26; Eph. 4: 1-8.

14. **Community/Supportive:** The recognition
and will to create a group of peers for the
purpose of ongoing mutual support and creative enhancement of each individual. The
additional awareness of the need for such a
group in the work environment and with
peer professionals to enable detachment
from external pressures that deter one from
acting with clarity on chosen values and ethical principles that might be otherwise compromised.

This value emerges from the understanding
of community in the early Church which
was based on the equal sharing of goods and
property. Understanding this ideal in the
context of modern culture enriches the
meaning of our experience of community as
supportive.

Eph. 4:1-16; Acts 2:44-45 and 4:32-5:10. (See
also Accountability/Ethics and Collabora-
tion/Subsidiarity.)

24. Courtesy/Hospitality: Offering polite and respectful treatment to others as well as treating guests and strangers in a friendly and generous manner. It also includes receiving the same treatment from others.
Peter 4:7-11.

41. Endurance/Patience: The ability to bear difficult and painful experiences, situations or people with calmness, stability and perseverance.
Book of Job and Heb. 10:32-39.

53. Generosity/Service: To share one's unique gifts and skills with others as a way of serving humanity without expecting reciprocation.
Luke 6:36-38 and 10:29-37; 1 Cor: 12 and 13.

75. Loyalty/Fidelity: Strict observance of promises and duties to those in authority and to those in close personal relationships.
Prov. 6:1-6; Eccl. 10:1-11; Luke 22:54-62; John 21; Rom. 3:20-31.

124. Worship/Faith/Creed: Reverence for and belief in God, that is expressed and experienced through a commitment to doctrines and teachings of religious belief. Worship gives "worth" or meaning to God as expressed so clearly in the Psalms.
Ps. 146-150; Ex. 30:30-35; John 4:20-24.

We all love differently according to our unique and special gifts. When a disciple loves within the context of Faith and Hope -- the spiritual connections -- the loved one feels not only the Love of the human disciple but the love of Christ through the emergence of the Spirit in the one who is loved. Although I was irritable after sitting with Rita for two days, she still felt loved through my gifts and values of Care/Nurture, Endurance/Patience and Community/Supportive.

Discipleship and the Struggle to Grow Spiritually

The gift of human consciousness makes possible a rich spiritual life. This has been the message of the mystics and sages of all ages. To reach the heights of spiritual potential requires discipline. Being a disciple means hoping for a new order in the world, where the values of God's kingdom reign rather than the values of human self-interest. Growing as a disciple is a struggle because developing Gospel values takes work.

Values form paths of spiritual development. They are connected and build upon each other to expand awareness of the meaning of Faith, Hope and Love. Three distinct paths relate to the Gospel values of Faith, Hope and Love.

[Self] ——————— **HOPE** ————▶ Ecority/
Preservation   Aesthetics

Security ————— **FAITH**————▶ Word

[Self]Interest——— **LOVE** ————▶ Intimacy/
                                                        Union

Each of these is a path of personal development. The values on the left are simple and straightforward and are experienced by most of us early in our life. But the values on the right are much more complex and develop over a period of time.

The **Hope Path** leads from [Self]Preservation where we see God as savior in a difficult world, to Ecority where we experience God as Lord of creation, a creation for which we are also responsible. Most of us have felt the need for [Self]Preservation at one time or another. When [Self]Preservation is a priority in our lives, we look to God for comfort in difficult times.

91. **[Self] Preservation:** Doing what is necessary to protect oneself from physical harm or destruction in an alien world.

Ps. 23, 31, 55 and 130; Matt. 6:25-34.

36. **Ecority/Aesthetics:** The capacity, skill, and personal, organizational or conceptual influence to enable persons to take authority for the created order of the world and to enhance its beauty and balance through creative technology in ways that have worldwide influence. In Genesis the concept that human beings are to be responsible for the earth develops into the concept that a new order of creation is being reborn.

Gen. 1: 26-30; Is. 2:6-9; Rom. 8:18-23; 2 Cor. 5: 17.

This is the value from Genesis that calls us to take authority for God's creation. The value is complex and involves working internationally to bring about a healthier planet in line with God's will. On the Hope Path an individual's need for [Self]Preservation can develop, over a lifetime, into ecority or preservation of the planet.

The **Faith Path** indicates a movement from Security, which is that very basic trust of others and the Lord, again at difficult times in our life. Security can be understood better by discussing its counterpart, insecurity, the feeling of anxiety each of us experiences. Anxiety is worry about the future, the belief that "something negative is going to happen, but I do not know what it is." Consider the definition of Security and the scripture that goes with it:

> **104. Security:** Finding a safe place or relationship where one experiences protection and is free from cares and anxieties.
>
> Ps. 23 and 91; Prov. 14:26; Matt. 6: 25-34.

Anxiety and insecurity are part of the human condition and a natural result of expectations about the future. Security is an internal feeling of comfort. Achievement/Success is an extension of Security and comfort, since it is a means of securing my future and avoiding insecurity. But consider what Jesus has to say about Security: "Therefore I tell you, do not be anxious about your life, what you shall eat or what you shall drink, not about your body, what you shall put on. Is not life more than food, and the body more than clothing?" (Matt. 6:25).

On the other end of this path is the very sophisticated and mysterious value of Word. Word is the experience of Christ that we discussed in the previous chapter. It is the high point of discipleship to live with this priority is one's life:

121. Word: The ability to communicate universal truths so effectively that the hearer becomes conscious of his/her limitations such that life and hope are renewed in the individual hearer.

Gen. 1; John 1:1-14; John 15; Acts 2:1-13; 1 John 1:1-4.

The **Love Path** is a movement from love as [Self]Interest/Control to love as Intimacy with God and God's Word.

63. [Self]Interest/Control: Restraining one's feelings and controlling one's personal interests in order to survive physically in the world.

1 John 2:29-34: 10; Heb. 10:32-39.

At the other end of the path is the wonderful experience of feeling that the Lord is present with one all the time. It is the experience of union with God that few, but some experience.

65. Intimacy and Solitude as Unitive: The experience of personal harmony that results from a combination of meditative practice, mutual openness and total acceptance of another person which leads to new levels of meaning and awareness of truth in unity with the universal order and connection with the Divine. The model for the western experience of mysticism and contemplative prayer is anticipated by this value.

John 17; Ps. 42:1-2, 46; Is. 26:1-19.

Hope: The Force to Preserve and to Create

The personal dimension of the Hope Path will be clearer as we become aware of the values between the two poles of [Self]Preservation and Ecority/Aesthetics. Any of the values can be substituted for other values similar in meaning. Therefore, the following is applicable to all the 125 values, but we use some of them here only as examples.

Survival is fundamental to all animal life. It requires adaptation to the demands of nature. Values such as [Self]Preservation, Safety/Survival and Food/Warmth/Shelter are extensions of survival. In the following diagram, [Self]Preservation develops into [Self]Worth. [Self]Worth emerges from the knowledge that I am valued by God and others. This is the Hope Path which becomes Gospel in value when Faith and Love are also present. It is only as I see that I am of value, of [Self]Worth, that my work comes alive and has purpose.

[Self] Worth Work — Service Art Corporation/New Order → **Ecority/**
Preservation **HOPE** **Aesthetics**

At the most basic level, Work is "doing and producing" in order to provide the necessities of life for my family and myself. Work/Labor, then, is doing and producing what is necessary for survival. To work I must cooperate with others, be skilled, and feel competent. Therefore, values such as [Self] Worth, [Self]Competence/Confidence and Education/Certification are all related to this path. These needs we call *foundation* needs, since they are the basic necessities of spiritual growth. When they are taken care of, and when Faith and Love are also in our lives, we are grasped by God's grace, Work/Labor is transformed to Service/Vocation.

>**106. Service/Vocation:** To be motivated to use one's unique gifts and skills to contribute to society through one's occupation, business, profession or calling.
>
>Matt. 6:1-4; 1 Cor. 12 and 13; Gal. 5:13-26.

This value is what Paul refers to as a "gift"(1 Cor. 12:4). As a Gospel value, Service/Vocation is the awareness that I have gifts that the community needs and that these gifts can contribute to the new order, which is the realization of Christ's dream of establishing the kingdom of God on earth.

At the far right of the continuum we encounter the need in each of us to create -- moving beyond procreation of children to creation of a new order. The value of Art as creativity for its own sake merges with Corporation/New Order and finally Ecority/Aesthetics. Ecority is the Gospel value of ecology that enables a person to see creation through divine eyes and work to enhance the created order. It is the mandate given in the Garden of Eden for humankind to take authority for the created order in line with God's plans. Care of the natural created order implies using technology and personal power in a responsible way. The value of Ecority/Aesthetics views humanity as a global family and the created order as our responsibility as co-creators with God. Humankind becomes the "chief gardener."

Faith: From Security to the Pursuit of Truth

In the Faith Path, the struggle is between the need for Security, Comfort and Control, and the need for meaning and the truth of God's Word. Between these two poles are other values:

Security ———— Worth Worship ● Search Faith Justice ——►Word

FAITH

Security is often linked with the need for [Self] Preservation, an obvious and strong connection. Theologically it is the bottom line of the Faith-Hope connection. Not so obvious is Security's role as a unique motivational force. [Self]Preservation is the legitimate reaction to a perceived external threat, while Security is an internal feeling of comfort and non-threat. When life is threatened, the natural reaction is to defend or fight back to preserve myself, but when I am in a state of constant insecurity I become more controlling.

Looking at the preceding diagram, we see that as we grow and mature, Security evolves into [Self] Worth. Extensions of [Self]Worth are [Self]Competence/Confidence, Achievement and Education as ways of being valued by others. This is just another way of pointing out how the values are all connected. There is another side to [Self]Worth which stems from curiosity or the need to know about things around me. The knowledge that others are valuable spawns in us -- from the very beginning of life -- a natural curiosity to understand the world outside. This aspect of [Self]Worth is connected to the other end of the continuum through a desire to search for the meaning of life (Search/Meaning). Worship is in fact a natural extension of [Self] Worth:

> **124. Worship/Faith/Creed:** Reverence for and belief in God, that is expressed and experienced through a commitment to doctrines and teachings of religious belief. Worship gives "worth" or meaning to God as expressed so clearly in the Psalms.
> Ps. 146-150; Ex. 30:30-35; John 4:20-24.

We see from the scriptural reference that original meaning of Worship was to honor God's "worth" just as we honor the "worth" of another person as an extension of our [Self]Worth. The time comes in our lives when we are seized by the higher Gospel values in the continuum. This is often known as conversion. Motivated now by the need for Meaning more than the need for Security, we actually become insecure when this new basic need to make sense out of life is not met. Faith/Risk/Vision now becomes the core of our life linked to the value of Word revealed to us in the person of Christ.

Recently during a counseling session a middle aged executive said to me, "I have been with this corporation for ten years and they have treated me very well. But I do not agree with a lot of their policies. They have offered me more money to stay but that just won't do it for me. I have got to move out on my own just to see what I can do." This sudden sense of new life and new direction is an experience of being *grasped by the future* as new possibilities open to us. It is an essential part of what the life of the disciple is about. More often than not, it is also a time of search for new meaning in one's life. Thus, at one end of the path we need Security while at the other we need the Security that comes from knowing and understanding what life, specifically my life, is about. To know what my life means is to discover its "meaning." Viktor Frankl speaks of the pull towards meaning: "Man's search for meaning is a primary force in his life and not a secondary rationalization of instinctual drives. This meaning is unique and specific in that it must and can be fulfilled by him alone; only then does it achieve a significance that will satisfy his own will to meaning."[4]

Another important aspect at this stage of development is the new sense of Equality and Justice that emerges. The person acquires a greater sense of others' rights. If my new sense of giftedness is growing in the hope dimension of my life then I must recognize my own equality. This in turn heightens my awareness of others' equality and their rights. Then there is a move from personal equality to the wider concept of concern for all oppressed people. The value that reflects this is Justice/Social Order:

> **67. Justice/Social Order:** Taking a course of action that addresses, confronts and helps correct conditions of human oppression in order to actualize the truth that every human being is of equal value.
>
> Prov. 2 1: 3; Micah 6:8; Matt. 5 and 23:23;

Rom. 3:5-6.

At this stage there is a newly found sense of independence. However, if independence does not include love and move to interdependence, it can lose its Gospel character and regress to a form of isolation and individualized power. When this happens the need for control and security once again predominates. The connection that allows independence to become interdependence is the value of Faith. Faith is related to Risk and Hope as vision and connects the disciple to this experience of Christ through God's Word.

> **47. Faith/Risk/Vision:** Behavioral commitment to values that are considered life-giving even at risk to one's life.
>
> Christ's faith was tested in the desert.
> Luke 4:1-13 and 9:18-21; Matt. 6:25-33; Rom. 1:8-9; Gal. 5:1-6; Heb. 12:1-12.

Love: From [Self]Interest to the Need for Intimacy

In this third path, tension exists between our need for control and our simultaneous need for love. Love includes being vulnerable and requires release of control. Because Love builds on the knowledge of the previous two paths, it is the most potent of the three.

Competition   Limitation

[Self] ——Family Fidelity——●——Empathy Dignity——▶ **Intimacy/**
Interest   **Union**

LOVE

Literature through the ages has shown us that

people have a tendency to feel they are the center of the universe and that everyone should cater to their needs. The value that reflects this is [Self]Interest/Control which stands behind the natural human tendency to be narcissistic. Erich Fromm describes narcissism "as a passion the intensity of which can only be compared with sexual desire and the desire to stay alive. In fact, many times it proves to be stronger than either."[5]

The word "narcissism" comes from the ancient Greek myth of Echo and Narcissus in which a self-centered youth, Narcissus, cruelly shuns the love of the nymph Echo. One day while sitting by a pool of water, he sees his image reflected in the water. Thinking the reflection is that of another nymph, he falls in love with it. Unable to have the person whose beauty he loves, he pines away and finally fades from existence. In his place grows a flower, purple within and white without, which forever commemorated his memory. Narcissism is a force within each of us quite distinct from survival and security needs.

Infants are born in this state of mind. They think they are the centers of the world. It is a natural state of narcissism. In fact, the human child is unique in the animal kingdom as needing the total attention of the mother in order to survive. From a theological point of view it is an experience of being of "infinite worth," our first awareness of God's grace. Maternal attention introduces us at the outset of life to the Gospel, the good news that each of us is of infinite value in the eyes of God.

The experience of conversion at this stage of the faith journey simply affirms in a conscious way not only our own infinite value but also the infinite value of others. In the absence of such awareness, narcissism become possession.

Early in life, we soon realize that if our demands for attention are to be met, some restraint is necessary. We thus learn to do as we are told for our own good, and we learn the necessity of discipline. In short, looking at the previous diagram, we learn what it means to live in a family (Family/Belonging) and to be loyal to others. One of the purposes of family is to procreate. It is where each of us finds love and nurturance. Thus equipped, we are able to grasp the Gospel vision of hope by becoming a co-creator with God of the world we live in, and caring for the family of humankind instead of surviving only in our immediate family.

As we continue to grow older, we learn that maturity demands that we reach out beyond ourselves to the wider range of peers and superiors we encounter at school and our place of work. We learn duty and loyalty (Loyalty/Fidelity) to our friends, to our primary institutions, and to our country. Like the early experience of narcissism, Competition has its positive side. It helps us confront our Limitations and trains us to see the values of others. It enables us to find our place and develop latent skills to their maximum potential. On the negative side, Competition can actually reinforce early feelings of narcissism and convince the winner that he or she is superior to other human beings. *At each and every point, it would seem that we can either grow spiritually or run the risk of regressing.*

At the midpoint when this Love is connected to Faith and Hope, conversion occurs again and we are grasped by God's grace and called to greater Intimacy with God and with those we love.

The process begins with the value of Empathy, which is the ability to project one's imagination into the imaginations of people, so they are able to see themselves with more clarity. This value of Empathy was the unique sign of Jesus of Nazareth. He entered the imagination of the poor in the Sermon on the Mount; he entered the imagination of each of the Apostles as he called them; he entered the imagination of the adulteress when he prevented her stoning; and he entered the imagination of each of us when he gave his life for us on the cross.

Empathy is the precursor to Human Dignity, the next value on the path. By taking on human flesh Jesus helped us see ourselves more clearly. In doing so, he dignified the human race.

The final point on the path is selfless giving in the act of Intimacy, something we all seek. Intimacy in its highest form between lovers brings with it a sense of union. We speak of the union between husband and wife as prefiguring the union between humans and God. The mystics constantly speak of this union with God as the very purpose of their lives. But behind Intimacy lies two other critical values: Limitation/Acceptance and Limitation/Celebration:

73. **Limitation/Acceptance:** Giving positive mental assent to the reality that one has boundaries and inabilities. This includes an objective self-awareness of one's strengths and potential, as well as weaknesses and inabilities. The capacity for self-criticism. This value describes the experience of forgiveness and reconciliation. As such it is also the narrative of Christ's passion -- his dying for our sins.

Matt. 8:21-22, chapters 26 and 27; Luke 15:11 -32, 23: 3-34; Rom. 3:21-26 and 5-8; Col. 1:19-20; Eph. 2:11-22; Mark 14-15; Luke 22 and 23; 1 Cor. 1:16-21 and 11:17-34.

74. **Limitation/Celebration:** The recognition that one's limits are the framework for exercising one's talents. The ability to laugh at one's own imperfections. Christ defeated our limitations, even the limitation of death and rose again. This is the value of personal growth and resurrection. It is expressed ritually through the act of communion or remembering the Lord's Supper.

Matt. 28; Mark 16; Luke 24; John 20-21; Acts 1:1-11; Rom. 5-8; Cor. 10:16-21 and 11:17-34.

These two values speak for themselves through the scriptural notes. They lie behind the ultimate act of Love, namely the death and resurrection of our Lord Jesus Christ. Incredible as it may seem, these same values also lie at the heart of all Christian Love. Therefore, they are central to each disciple's life. A willingness to be vulnerable finally leads to union in any act of Intimacy, whether it be husband and wife or union with God. Evelyn Underhill, a great scholar of the mystics, notes that what made Christian mystics exceptional was their recognition of the relationship between divine and human intimacy. "In theoretical language, their theory of knowledge is that the spirit of man, itself essentially divine, is capable of immediate communion with God, the One Reality."[6]

Conclusion

We have examined three paths; Faith, Hope and Love. On each path we face a struggle between the natural inclinations within us to be more self-centered and the need to be open to each other and to the Other, who is Christ. However, only as we see these forces as a whole do we realize their full implications. The 125 values connect to form patterns that help us discern God's plan for using our unique gifts. This raises the issue of call. Like the early disciples each of us is called to be a part of God's plan. This is the subject of the next chapter.

Chapter 4

Paths on the Faith Journey: Discerning God's Call

As Jesus passed along the sea of Galilee, he saw Simon and his brother Andrew casting a net into the sea --for they were fishermen. And Jesus said to them, "Follow me and I will make you fish for people." Immediately they left their nets and followed him. As he went a little farther, he saw James son of Zebedee and his brother John who were in their boats mending nets. Immediately he called them; and they left their father Zebedee in the boat with the hired men, and followed him.

Mark 1:16-20

We are on the edge of a new age of discovery, an age of convergence between the inner world of the human mind and the spirit. New understandings of how the human brain works would suggest that three-dimensional images occur at an unconscious level prior to any human action. These images prefigure all that we do before we do it. The brain, then, is a kind of inner architectural planning room. Contrary to some popular psychology, it may not be the past that is the primary influence on our lives, but that which calls us from the future.

We have seen in earlier chapters how values are signs and mediators between the inner world of images and the external, observable world of everyday life. Our values stand between these two worlds as a way of understanding both our inner life and our external behavior. Therefore values, more than anything, are a very important source of information about our spiritual lives and what it is God calls us to. Values actually connect us with the future, with what it is that God wants us to be and become.

Each disciple is on a journey, on a path that is unique and different from any other disciple's path. Like the first disciples, Jesus calls us to fulfill a special mission or contribution, based on our own unique abilities. In this chapter we will explore ways to learn more about our special missions and our own unique contributions. We will begin by examining the fact that values cluster in patterns. These patterns provide valuable information about ourselves and what God calls us to do or to be.

Mapping the Disciple's Faith Journey

To learn more about our values, we can look at them developmentally to see how they grow and change throughout our lives. When we look at values in this way, we begin to see both the gifts of the values and the potential of those gifts for future growth.

The following Faith Map presents values developmentally.[1] The Faith Map may look a bit intimidating at first, just as the map of a foreign country may be intimidating (especially if it is written in a language we don't understand), but as we work through the different sections of the map, we will be able to read and understand it. The Faith Map is a visual way of "mapping" our faith journeys, of seeing our current place on the journey and discerning how to grow spiritually. The Faith Map is a road map for our personal spiritual journeys. Let's begin by getting "the lay of the land."

PHASE I

A GOALS	B GOALS
[Self]Interest/ Control [Self]Preservation Wonder/Awe/ Fate	Security Physical Delight

A MEANS	B MEANS
Food/Warmth/ Shelter Function/ Physical Safety/Survival	Affection/Physical Economics/Profit Property/Control Sensory Pleasure/ Sex Territory/Security Wonder/Curiosity

PHASE II

A GOALS	B GOALS
Family/Belonging Fantasy/Play [Salf]Worth	[Self]Competence Play/Recreation Work/Labor Worship/Faith/ Creed

A MEANS	B MEANS
Being Liked Care/Nurture Control/Order/ Discipline Courtesy/ Hospitality Dexterity/ Coordination Endurance/ Patience Friendship/ Belonging	Achievement/ Success Administration/ Control Economics/ Success Education/ Certification Hierarchy/ Propriety Law/Rule Loyalty/Fidelity

PHASE IV

B GOALS	A GOALS
Ecority/Aesthetics Transcendence/ Equality Word	Intimacy and solitude as Unitive Truth/Wisdom/ Insight

B MEANS	A MEANS
Convivial Technology Human Rights/ World Justice/ Distribution Macroeconomics Minessence	Community/ Personalist Detachment/ Transcendence Interdependence Prophet/Vision Synergy

PHASE III

B GOALS	A GOALS
Construction/ New Order Human Dignity Justice/Social Order Presence/Dwelling Faith/Risk/Vision	Equality/ Liberation Integration/ Wholeness Life/Self- Actualization Service/Vocation

B MEANS	A MEANS
Accountability/ Ethics Community/ Supportive Growth/Expansion Intimacy Creativity/Idea Limitation/ Celebration Mission/Objectives Simplicity/Play	Equity/Rights Empathy Health/Healing Independence Law/Guide Limitation/ Acceptance Search/Meaning/ Hope Sharing/Listening/ Trust

Reading the Faith Map

The map is divided into phases, stages (A and B in each phase), goals and means.

Phases: When we look at a road map, we usually begin by looking at the large geographical entities such as countries or states. On the Faith Map the largest entities are the phases: Phase I, Phase II, Phase III and Phase IV. The values in the later phases grow from, or build upon, the values of the earlier phases. The phases of consciousness are developmental; that is, they appear in a particular order and sequence, from childhood to maturity.

The phases represent different periods in the development of our spiritual life. In each phase we look at the world and God in a different way. It is not God that changes, but our perception of God alters as we mature spiritually. A similar thing happens to a child within a family. As the child grows to maturity, his or her relationships with other members of the family, particularly the parents, develop and change. As the baby becomes a child, a teenager and finally an adult, he/she sees other family members in varying ways.

First, the child perceives the parents as sources of protection and security. As the child approaches adolescence, however, the family becomes less important and sometimes even the object of rebellion. Finally, as the adolescent approaches maturity, he/she experiences a growing appreciation for the family.

We are like the children whose view of their parents grows with appreciation the older we get.

So it is in our relationship with God.

On the maps you will notice that there is a boundary between each of the phases, just as borders mark the boundaries of countries. As we travel on our faith journeys, we generally travel in a circular manner, rather than in a straight line. (This is depicted on the Faith Map as movement in a clockwise direction: you will experience Phase I first, move on to Phase II, then go to Phase III and finally to Phase IV.)

As life circumstances change and as we develop new skills for living, our values also change. We often move backward and forward through the phases during different periods of our lives. Yet, on our return visits, we are not likely to experience the phases as we did before. As we grow, we acquire new skills. When we return to a previously experienced phase, we bring those newly acquired skills with us.

Stages: Next you will notice smaller entities, somewhat like cities on a road map. These are called stages. Each stage has several values listed under it. Stage A values are personal values, that is, values we live out in our personal lives. Stage B values are ones we live out primarily in institutional settings, such as work, church, school, or government.

Goal Values: Where We Want to Go and Who We Want to Be

If you are a keen map reader, you've probably already noticed that the stages are divided into two sections. The top section contains values called "Goal" values. These values develop at specific points in our lives, and we continue to hold them throughout our lives. Goal values are important to us; our "goal" is to keep them fully incorporated in our lives. Although we hold our goal values all our lives, as we grow, change and develop new skills, our goal values change in complexity and quality. Our values change as we change; they grow as we grow.

Means Values: The Ways We Achieve Our Goals

The bottom section under each stage lists "Means" values. These are skills values, values that help us achieve our goal values. For example, just as the skill of driving a car is a means by which we reach our destination on a cross-country trip, the means (or skill) value of Care/Nurture enables us to achieve our goal value of Family/Belonging. Caring for and nurturing family members helps us fulfill our desire for good family relationships.

You will notice that the lists of Means values are longer than the lists of Goal values. This reflects the fact that there are many different means, skills, methods, ways that different people use to reach the same long-term goal. The same is true when several different people plan a trip to the same destination: one will drive, another will take a plane or a train, a third person may hitchhike or walk. The goal is the same; the means to reach that goal differs with the individual.

Spiritual Development and the Four Phases

In the last chapter we looked at the three paths of Gospel value development related to Faith, Hope and Love. Those paths all began in Phase I and continue into Phase IV, as shown on the Faith Map. Now let's take a closer look at the Faith Map, this time exploring the development of the different phases.

The values we hold are signs of God's action in our lives. Each phase contains its own particular information. The phase in which a person's Gospel values are found, reveals knowledge about the person's perception of the world as well as that person's faith orientation or consciousness. In order to find meaning and to cope with the world around us, we construct a perception of the world, a world-view, and an image of what it means for us to function effectively in that world, a self-image.

For example, some people see the world as an unsafe, unfriendly place (their world-view) over which they have no control (their self-image). Their faith in others is minimal causing them to rely on God as a savior from a difficult world. Others see the world as a project, a place where there is much work to be done (world-view), and they see themselves as active participants in accomplishing this work (self-image). Their faith tends to be placed in their ability to save themselves through their work or works.

These world-views and self-images are also forms of faith consciousness, because they deal with how we know and experience God, ourselves and the world. The content of our world-views and self-images change significantly as we mature because the phases of consciousness are developmental and sequential.

We must satisfactorily experience each phase before moving into another. At the same time, our values change, and we grow spiritually. There are differences in the values held by men and women in different phases. Hence, the gifts of men and women differ at different times of their lives. Each phase has its own distinct character.[2] Let's take a look now at how some of those distinctive characteristics.

PHASE I

A GOALS	B GOALS
[Self]Interest/Control [Self]Preservation Wonder/Awe/Fate	Security Physical Delight

A MEANS	B MEANS
Food/Warmth/Shelter Function/ Physical Safety/Survival	Affection/Physical Economics/Profit Property/Control Sensory pleasure/ Sex Territory/ Security Wonder/Curiosity

Phase I: During the initial phase, we seek to satisfy physical needs: food, warmth, shelter. The need for [Self]Preservation and Security motivates us to acquire skills that will guarantee our Safety and ensure our Survival.

In Phase I, we view the world as an alien place over which we have no control. For children, this means the world is full of mystery to which they respond with Wonder and Awe. Adults in this phase see the world as hostile and unfriendly, a place in which they merely exist. They have unmet needs, and life is a constant struggle. People in leadership roles tend to be autocratic and controlling.

Phase I experiences provide the foundation of our Faith. On the positive side, we experience Christ as a personal savior who helps us in a difficult world. Childhood experiences that nurture Love and Faith are important for future spiritual development. On the negative side, there is a tendency to see God or Christ as distant and removed from our lives. This view makes God a last resort in difficult times.

PHASE II

A GOALS	B GOALS
Family/Belonging	[Self]Competence
Fantasy/Play	Play/Recreation
[Self]Worth	Work/Labor
	Worship/Faith/Creed

A MEANS	B MEANS
Being Liked	Achievement/Success
Care/Nurture	Administration/Control
Control/Order	Economics/Success
Courtesy/Hospitality	Education/Certification
Dexterity/Coordination	Hierarchy/Propriety
Endurance/Patience	Law/Rule
Friendship/Belonging	Loyalty/Fidelity

Phase II: Our view of the world is problematic, but we believe with hard work and persistence, we will be able to cope. During this phase, we learn to do things which merit the approval of significant people. This guarantees our acceptance within the groups important to us and enhances our own sense of competence and confidence. Adults in Phase II strive to conform to the norms of significant people and groups in our lives. By becoming productive, we satisfy our social needs for acceptance, affirmation, approval and achievement. Rules and attention to law is important to us. Leadership at this stage tends to be either very parental or hierarchical in its style.

By experiencing belonging and success, we realize a sense of [Self]Worth at this phase, especially by belonging to established institutions like the church. Women in Phase II tend to place personal (IIA) values as a first priority. This means women stress the relational and interpersonal side of life. Men, on the other hand, emphasize IIB values. As a consequence, men are more competitive and less caring, more concerned about rules and structure and less concerned about emotional issues.

During Phase II we learn the basic tenets of our faith, the meaning and importance of Scripture and the place of worship in our lives. Faith develops by belonging to and learning from a faith community. Very often this is the faith community of home and family. We see God as the external being that created the universe. However, we see Christ as master and teacher in very human terms. Christ is the teacher from whom we must learn, rather than a mystery over which we have no control. Because we see the world not only as problematic but also as something with which we can cope, learning about our Lord through Scripture and study is essential.

The Transition Stage

In the course of spiritual development it is quite common to be in-between the first and last two phases. Phases I and II are essentially the foundation stages when we grow in discipleship by forming a relationship with God, through learning about Scripture and by trusting the faith community. We learn to trust God as saviour and teacher and learn to love God, among other ways, through public worship.

Phases III and IV: These two phases build upon this foundation and become the focus of ministry and call. Here our spiritual orientation is directed inward. God becomes an interior friend. Personal prayer is emphasized and supplemented by public worship rather than the other way around. Scripture is very important, but in a more personal way, as we seek guidance for our unique mode of ministry and service.

The value differences of men and women flow into the last two phases, but in a more integrated form. Women, for example, tend to place Justice as a top priority with lesser attention to the pursuit of Truth. Men have the same values but tend to reverse the priorities.

PHASE III

B GOALS	A GOALS
Construction/New Order	Equality/Liberation
Human Dignity	Integration/Wholeness
Justice/Social Order	Life/Self-Actualization
Presence/Dwelling	Service/Vocation
Faith/Risk/Vision	

B MEANS	A MEANS
Accountability/Ethics	Equity/Rights
Community/Supportive	Empathy
Growth/Expansion	Health/Healing
Intimacy	Independence
Creativity/Ideas	Law/Guide
Limitation/Celebration	Limitation/Acceptance
Mission/Objectives	Search/Meaning/Hope
Simplicity/Play	Sharing/Listening

Phase III: In this phase the world-view shifts toward the perception of the world as a creative project to which we can contribute. A concern for the quality of life emerges, leading us to focus our activity on ensuring human rights and justice in the social order, or on improving the conditions for personal growth in the institutions within which we function. When we begin to act on Phase III values, we no longer need the affirmation of others to realize our self-worth, and we no longer find meaning in living up to the expectations of others. Instead we find meaning in revitalizing, even reshaping, the institutions of which we are a part and in accepting responsibility for that revitalization.

The transition into a Phase III faith usually does occur before early adulthood, and it can occur any time during adulthood. During this phase, spirituality focuses on the inner dimension of meaning, making personal prayer and contemplation more important than public worship. Now the foundation of our faith becomes a personal inner experience of conversation, and a daily walking and talking with the Lord. Christ is now experienced as friend. We also experience the Holy Spirit working as a friend within us. With relation to the community, we see ourselves as having special God-given gifts that the community needs. We are motivated by personal needs to express our discipleship within the Body of Christ, to be our authentic selves, to direct our lives and to live the vision of hope that Christ has given us through our special and unique gifts.

PHASE IV

B GOALS

Ecority/Aesthetics
Transcendence/Equality
Word

A GOALS

Intimacy and Solitude as
    Unitive
Truth/Wisdom/Insight

B MEANS

Convivial Technology
Human Rights/World
Justice/Distribution
Macroeconomics
Minessence

A MEANS

Community/Personalist
Detachment/Transcendence
Interdependence
Prophet/Vision
Synergy

Phase IV: The world is viewed as an unfinished, incomplete work, a mystery needing care. In this phase, we see the world's present condition as less important than its future potentiality. However, this does not imply a disregard or lack of concern for people or communities, because they too are viewed in their potentiality as well as in their actuality.

In this phase, our perception of the world expands dramatically. This expanded perception enters our consciousness as a series of tasks to be performed. This work is done in conjunction with other like-minded people in order to bring about a better world, where the needs of the most deprived are met. We become change-agents and see ourselves as cooperating in the on-going act of creation.

Working with others reveals another interesting and crucial aspect of Phase IV. The individual self is transcended and we act interdependently with other "selves." The "I" becomes "we." This "we" includes not only humankind but nature as well. In this common, interdependent collaboration and action among women, men and nature itself, a unity begins to emerge between humankind and technology. We see technology, now so widely available and accessible, as a tool for positive contributions. Phase IV consciousness uses technology to create global cooperation, collaboration -- and ultimately to create global unity.

Two values, which we have not seen before, help illustrate Phase IV. First, Human Rights/ World Social Order involves committing oneself and using talent, education, training and resources to create the means for all people to achieve just access to adequate food, habitat, employment, health and minimal practical education.

The second value, Justice/Global Distribution, reflects a commitment to the fact that all people have equal value, but also recognizes that people have different gifts and abilities to contribute to society. This recognition of the value, gifts and abilities of all people combines with a capacity to elicit collaboration among institutions and governments that will help provide the basic life necessities for the poor.

At Phase IV we experience a personal yet universal Christ which radically shifts our orientation toward the world from being self-centered to other-centered. We begin to see the world through Christ's eyes and choose to revere and enhance the environment in accordance with God's plans for the created order. The self is transcended as the individual "I" becomes a community "we" within the Body of Christ. Here we live out the call to humankind to renew the face of the earth. The world is seen as a mystery for which we share and take responsibility with the Creator.

The Four Phases: A Summary

The phases, including Stages A and B within each phase, are an all-encompassing attitudinal framework within which we make meaning out of our world. At Phase I, we seek to satisfy our physical needs for food, warmth, shelter, pleasure and sex. Then at Phase II, the social needs for acceptance, affirmation, approval and achievement emerge. At Phase III, we seek to satisfy the personal need to express creative insights, be ourselves, direct our lives and own our ideas and enterprises. Finally, at Phase IV we seek, with like-minded people to satisfy the communal need for global harmony. We do this by nurturing people and communities in order to create a better and more just world in harmony with God's will for all of creation. While each phase is a partial consciousness of the whole and the mystery of God, Phase IV is more integrated, and in its complexity encompasses the other three phases.

The Disciple's Path of Spiritual Development: Foundation to Future

The four phases and eight stages of consciousness reflect each person's unique faith journey. The faith journey can be represented in a Faith Map, as shown earlier in this chapter. How does the Faith Map work? As part of a program that my associates and I have developed, a person completes a questionnaire. The responses indicate his/her values. When the responses are tabulated and analyzed mathematically, it is possible to determine where in Phase I, II, III or IV the person's values lie.

Throughout the development of the program, studies were carried out to determine if, in fact, the results shown on participants' Faith Maps accurately reflected their values and phase of consciousness. These studies confirmed both the validity of the questionnaire and our process of evaluating it.[3]

More than five thousand people have now completed the questionnaire and examined their values in this way. People often ask what stage or phase they are in. Although it is natural to be curious about this, my associates and I discovered that knowing the values priorities and where these are located on the Faith Map is more important than knowing the phase or stage. We found that people typically have values in every stages of development. The following Faith Map of an individual illustrates what I mean.

PHASE I

A GOALS   **B GOALS**

[Self]Interest/   Security
Control

A MEANS   **B MEANS**

          Affection/Physical
          Economics/Profit

PHASE II

A GOALS   **B GOALS**

[Self]Worth   [Self]
                 Competence
                 Worship/Faith/
                 Creed

A MEANS   **B MEANS**

Being Liked   Economics/
Courtesy/   Success
   Hospitality   Education/
Friendship/   Certification
   Belonging   Hierachary/
                 Propriety
                 Achievement/
                 Success
                 Productivity
                 Administration

PHASE IV

B GOALS   **A GOALS**

Word   Truth/ Wisdom/
                 Insight

B MEANS   **A MEANS**

Human Rights/   Prophet/Vision
   World

PHASE III

B GOALS   **A GOALS**

Faith/Risk/   Life/Self-
Vision   Actualization
                 Integration/
                 Wholeness
                 Service/
                 Vocation

B MEANS   **A MEANS**

Community/   Equity/Rights
   Supportive   Independence
Mission/   Law/Guide
   Objective   Search/Meaning/
                 Hope
                 Sharing/
                 Listening/Trust

This typifies what any person will find, namely that each of us has values in all of the phases, rather than just in one. You can see by looking at the Faith Map that the greatest concentration for this person is in Phase IIB and IIIA. But what about the other values? How do they fit into life? Values fall into three categories that parallel our spiritual development: Foundation, Focus and Future (or Call).

At the beginning of Mark, we hear the story of Jesus calling the first disciples: "As he went a little farther, he saw James, son of Zebedee, and his brother John who were in their boats mending nets. Immediately he called them"(1:19). If we look at the passage in Mark just prior to this we read: "Jesus came to Galilee, proclaiming the good news of God and saying," 'The time is fulfilled and the kingdom of God has come near, repent and believe in the good news" (1:14).

Here Jesus proclaims the message of Hope we spoke about in the last chapter. The kingdom is the new order; the twelve apostles represent the new Israel, which will nurture the values that will bring the possibility of resurrection and love to all people. "Repent" means to change your ways and live the Faith -- live now as if God's kingdom were already here. Jesus called the disciples to act out a hopeful future. Call is an invitation to the future. Jesus called or invited the disciples to join him because they had special gifts, values and talents that Jesus recognized. He asked them to commit these gifts to the development of the Kingdom. Just as Jesus called the disciples long ago, Jesus calls us to develop the Kingdom. He calls each of us personally. Our unique values contain the elements of this call. Let me illustrate with a story from my own life.

A Personal Conversion Experience.

When I was in my mid-twenties, I immigrated to Canada. I landed in Montreal with no money and lived from hand to mouth until I finally got a job and earned enough money to hitchhike to Vancouver. I was so poor that I lived in one room and ate in Salvation Army shelters for several months. Finally, desperately lonely, I decided to go to a local church to meet some people. Gradually I made friends, and with their help I found a job as a trainee in a chemical laboratory.

After meeting a university professor who encouraged me to take night classes and write the provincial examination for British Columbia, which would gain me entrance to the university, I stopped going to church. It appeared that finally my life was coming together. Then one Saturday evening, sitting alone, I felt very despondent. "What now?" I thought. An internal response seemed to say, "It is time to go to church." I checked to see the time that services were held in the little rural parish outside the town of New Westminster where I was staying. Sunday's service was to begin at 8:30 a.m.

The next morning when I told the friends with whom I stayed that I was going to church, they were sure I had the wrong time -- that services were later in the morning. I assured them I had read the notice correctly, but when I arrived at the church, the parking lot was empty and no one was there! The church notice said the service was at eleven o'clock. Furious with myself I started to walk home. Then, once again, I heard that inner voice. "Go into the church," it seemed to say.

A little fearful that I was hearing things, I went up to the church, opened the main door and looked in. Walking towards me was the minister, a short stocky man, with kind eyes that looked through thick-lensed, tortoiseshell rimmed spectacles. He beckoned to me. As I approached him, he simply said, "Don't preoccupy yourself, young man. You have been called by God to ministry!" I spent the next three days walking and talking to him about the meaning of "call." It seemed impossible to me that God could want me for anything. The minister excited me about seminary and studies, about becoming a missionary to foreign lands and helping those in need.

A year later I went to college and after that to seminary. Several years after that, I went to Barrio Cuba in Costa Rica where my work on values really began. When I look now at my ministry in research and teaching, I can trace it all back to that one voice in the church saying "You have been called by God to ministry!" As I look at my own values now I can still see that call in my values today, but I also see other things that might help us understand more fully the spiritual path of the disciple.

The Foundation, Focus, and Future of Our Faith

The following diagram is an approximation of what my Faith Map would have looked like after I entered seminary. (It is an approximation, of course, because the process we are using to identify and group values into phases did not exist at that time.)

As we see, my values are focused into three areas. The values in Phase IIB and III A are called Focus Values, which detail what I was focusing on daily -- namely succeeding in my education, growing in the faith and training for ministry or Service/Vocation. Focus Values are the strongest grouping of values, the "focus" of most of our daily activities. Therefore these are the values that require the greatest output of time and energy. They also form our world-view, the perspective from which we see ourselves in relation to the world around us.

PHASE I

A GOALS

[Self] Preservation
Wonder/Awe/Fate

B GOALS

Security

A MEANS

Food/Warmth/Shelter
Safety/Survival

B MEANS

Affection/Physical
Economics/Profit

FOUNDATION VALUES

PHASE IV

B GOALS

Transcendence/Equality
Word

A GOALS

Intimacy and Solitude
  as Unitive
Truth/Wisdom/Insight

B MEANS

Human Rights/World
Justice/Distribution

A MEANS

Interdependence
Prophet/Vision

FUTURE (or CALL) VALUES

PHASE II

A GOALS

Family/ Belonging
[Self] Worth

A MEANS

Being Liked
Care/Nurture
Courtesy/Hospitality
Endurance/Patience
Friendship/Belonging

B GOALS

[Self] Competence
Worship/Faith/Creed

B MEANS

Achievement/Success
Economics/Success
Education/Certification
Hierarchy/Propriety
Loyalty/Fidelity

FOCUS VALUES

PHASE III

B GOALS

Justice/Social Order
Presence/Dwelling
Faith/Risk/Vision

B MEANS

Community/Supportive
Growth/Expansion
Leisure/Freesence
Limitation/Celebration
Mission/Objectives

A GOALS

Equality/Liberation
Life/Self-Actualization
Service/Vocation

A MEANS

Equity/Rights
Independence
Law/Guide
Search/Meaning/Hope
Sharing/Listening/Trust

All the values that precede the Focus area, namely those in Phase IA and IB and Phase IIA, are called Foundation Values. On my Faith Map, they are the values that I had put in place before I went to seminary. These values represent the basic necessities of life. While these basics differ for each of us, they provide the basics needed for spiritual growth and development. Our Foundation Values provide the structure or the "foundation" on which the Focus Values are later developed. They contribute to making each of us the unique child of God that we are. They also assist us as we seek to live a life of discipleship.

All the values that follow the Focus Values, Phase IIIB to IVB, contain the gifts that you are called or invited to use for the Kingdom. They are our Future Values, God's invitation to us as unique individuals. Future Values energize and inspire us to live out our Focus Values each day. They are the signs of God's call and are the primary motivators in our spiritual lives. When I look at the values in the Future area of my Faith Map, I see the value of Word so central to the work I talked about in Barrio Cuba in chapter 2, as well as values like Community/Support, Prophet/Vision and Justice/Social Order. These values continue to inform my life, but it is important for me to remember that they were activated by another Christian who identified God's plan for me and asked me to respond.

The Discernment of Spirits: Values as Questions

Our values nurture our inner lives. They are one of the special ways in which the Spirit talks to us. The minister who activated my call in a sense called forth this potential in me. In other words our values are seeds of the spirit -- each disciple has them. But as we move along in our faith journeys, we often find that the Spirit doesn't always talk with us directly or give us specific advice. Instead, the Spirit relies on all the gifts God has given us: emotions, intellect, bodies, values. These often raise questions that we must explore in order to discover or discern the movement of God in our lives.

A series of questions, which we call discernment questions, can be addressed to each of our values. ("discernment" or "discernment of spirits" are ancient Christian terms used to name the process of recognizing or "discerning" the movement of God in our lives.) Discernment questions help us explore our values, the ways they affect our day-to-day behavior and the steps needed to integrate them more fully into our lives. When we engage in this process, we are discerning God's plans for us.

Discernment questions flow naturally from our values as they are reflected in Scripture. For example as you review the values in the appendix, perhaps you find [Self]Worth is a priority value for you. Among other scriptural passages, John 3: 16 expresses this value. God loves and esteems us so much that Jesus became human as we are in order to save us. [Self]Worth in Christian terms is accepting the gift of the incarnation in Jesus Christ.

The value of [Self]Worth suggests that we are of great worth. Scripture confirms that God loves us so much that God's son became human on our account to save and deliver us. This combination raises these questions for us to consider:

- Do I recognize how much God loves me?
- Do I behave as if God loves me in the way I love others?

The values that we identify as our own, together with related Scripture naturally raise important discernment questions for us. Let us take another example.

Perhaps you have identified Search/Meaning/Hope (103) as one of your values. You consider it important to integrate your feelings, imagination and objective knowledge in order to discover your unique place in the world. The Scripture -- particularly Luke 11:19-13 and Romans 8:24-27 -- assures you that God is listening and will respond. Discernment questions that come naturally from this might include:

- Are you sharing your thoughts and search with others in the faith community?
- Are you reflecting on the Scripture in such a way that God knows you are searching and asking for a response?
- Is there hope in your life?
- Do you see the gifts that you have to offer, have you asked others you trust what your gifts are?

In spiritual discernment the answers are not as

important as the questions that the spirit puts to us through our values. Why? Because open-ended questions such as these lead us to pursue our call continually. Questions generate insight. They can also reveal God's active presence with us in our day-to-day experiences. For example if I tell you that you are miserable today, you might object because it does not capture exactly what you feel. But on the otherhand, if I say, "Are you feeling sad or a little miserable today?" You are more likely to reflect on what it is I am saying.

When discernment questions arise, responses to them should be confirmed by our own experience and by what others tell us about ourselves. Christian life is a communal experience; we are all a part of the Body of Christ. Because of this, the community can often assist us as we seek to understand God's action in our life. After I said "yes" to the call to ministry, I had to evaluate my life and ask others if they felt this was an appropriate direction for me knowing me as they did.

The Spirit most often moves through community. In your own life have you ever felt that it was time to pursue a new job, to use gifts that you had ignored before or that you now felt ready to use? If so, then you probably checked out any remaining doubts with a special friend or a spiritual guide -- someone who knows you well and whose integrity you trust. More than likely, this person told you something that removed your doubts, validated your feelings and strengthened your resolve about making a change. This helped confirm that God was moving in your feelings about making a job change.

Conclusions

Up to this point we have explored the ways the 125 values are connected and form patterns that enable us to discern God's plans for us and our unique gifts. This raises the issue of "call," the fact that like the early disciples, each of us is also invited to be active in God's plan. We also looked at the idea of discernment. The original concept of discernment of spirits recognized that we live in a world that is a battleground between good and evil. We found that by asking "discernment questions" about our values, we can begin to discover the "good" in our lives. That is, we can see where God is present and moving in our lives.

The link that unifies these seemingly separate elements is the dimension of church as the Body of Christ. Each of us develops in relationship to our primary institutions. We are individuals within systems rather than people in isolation. When the need for survival, security and narcissism are connected through institutional pressures, the force of evil is unleashed in ways that are beyond the power of the individual to cope with. On the other hand, when intimacy, truth, and harmony are connected through a loving institution or community, an equal force to the good is mobilized. These forces become the central tension in personal spiritual discernment and are the subject matter of the next chapter.

Chapter 5

The Disciple's Struggle with Good and Evil

*Then war broke out in heaven. Michael and his
angels battled against the dragon. Although the
dragon and his angels fought back, they were
overpowered and lost their place in heaven. The
huge dragon, the ancient serpent known as the devil
or Satan, the seducer of the whole world was driven
out: he was hurled down to the earth and his
minions with him.*

Revelation 12:7-9

This chapter examines our struggle as disciples with good and evil, depicted so well in the quotation from the book of Revelation above. We have seen how in our individual struggles to grow in life-giving ways we are constantly pulled in two directions. One direction is life-giving for ourselves and others, while the opposite is destructive and self-serving. At the heart of this struggle is living in community -- institutional living -- which in Christian terms is the life in the Body of Christ.

Institutional living is inherent in our lives as human beings. Without civil institutions order and all its attributes would not exist. From the institution of family emerges the possibility of love. From the institution of the church grows the possibility of resurrection. Yet at the same time, as most of us know, institutions can be coercive, tension-producing and even destructive. Families are broken by divorce. The church has had the Inquisition and corrupt tele-evangelists. We know that Christ died for us and the victory is ours, but still we struggle each day with good and evil.

For the disciple, hope and the possibility of exceptional service (mission) and spiritual growth occur within the context of community. The basic unit of Christian society is the Body of Christ, the faith community. Paul is clear that this is where our gifts are nurtured. He uses the analogy of the human body to illustrate his point: "For just as the body is one and has many members, and all the members of the body, though many, are one body, so it is with Christ"(1 Cor. 12:12). Later in the same chapter,

Paul expands the thought even more, "If one member suffers, all suffer together with it; if one member is honored, all rejoice together with it. Now you are the body of Christ and individually members of it" (vv. 26-27).

The paths of Faith, Hope and Love are interlaced and connected with all values, and they are part of each phase of spiritual development. These three paths lie at the heart of the Christian disciple's ability to grow in love. Institutions provide a primary way to express this love. If an institution is connected with the paths of Faith, Hope and Love, it can help release the infinite possibility of love in each of us. But institutions can also be the tools of evil. This was the case when people and institutions backed Hitler. The horrible result was the Holocaust. However, when an institution intentionally becomes an instrument for love the very opposite occurs. How this intentional action leads to good rather than to evil is the subject of this chapter.

The Spiritual Paths

The following diagram from chapter 3 will remind us of the three spiritual paths.

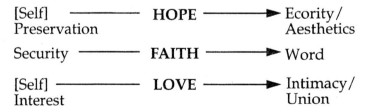

[Self] Preservation	———	HOPE	———▶	Ecority/ Aesthetics
Security	———	FAITH	———▶	Word
[Self] Interest	———	LOVE	———▶	Intimacy/ Union

We looked at these three paths as paths of individual spiritual growth, and we have noted that for values to be Gospel values, the element of Love and Faith must be related to Hope. Through Hope, the Kingdom of God is gradually actualized in human life. Hope is the vision that encompasses the spread of justice to and the experience of human dignity by all people. This vision is first realized in individuals and then in the faith community. Finally, then, the Kingdom of God is actualized in the world through institutions. Our faith is acted out by the manner in which we love one another in institutional settings. We are now going to revisit the paths of Faith, Hope and Love looking at them as institutional rather than personal experiences.

Path One: The Church as Institution -- Hope

At the purely institutional level, work and production are the normal way we preserve ourselves on a daily basis. A serious mission needs an institution to support it and enable it to happen. Institutionally this is what this path is about.

Since the death of Christ, the institutional Church has enabled hope throughout most societies. For example, modern medicine, social services and education have grown out of the creativity and vision of Hope that the Church has provided down through the centuries in the Western world.

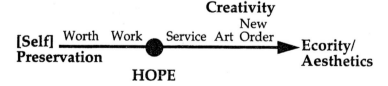

94

When an organization is not financially viable, pressure is put on the employees to work harder and produce more. (Clergy often work endless hours because their sense of worth is closely tied to their work. They rarely have a direct boss and often feel obligated to please everyone in the congregation.) As an institution grows, becomes financially stable ([Self]Preservation) and well established, it is able to sponsor creative opportunity for its personnel and begins to see itself as a service to the community. In Christian terms, the Church, which began with the first disciples as we see in Acts, was established through the leadership of apostles. The value of Construction/New Order became a reality and the young Church was able to exercise its mission to renew the earth (Ecority/Aesthetics). This remains the Church's mission today.

Path Two: Communal Accountability -- Faith

On this second path (Faith), institutional security and control are promoted through administration and management procedures. The more insecure the leadership, the more rigid the management design. This is common in struggling family businesses -- or congregations -- where management is a one-person affair. Responsible controls and efficient planning are essential for any institution's continued development.

Security — Worth Worship — Search Faith Justice → Word

FAITH

As the institution grows, Security is built in through the creation of friendships and on-going support groups. Full participation in the institution is critical role for the disciple today, just as it was for the first apostles. As more people are given real Authority, this allows Independence and demands faith and risk as well as Mutual Responsibility. The ultimate exercise of one's authority involves the cultivation of new ideas. Thus, institutional authority as a system of respect requires study, scholarship and the search for truth (Word) and the struggle for meaning (Search/Meaning/Hope) and Justice.

Path Three: Institution and Human Dignity -- Love

The most basic institution in society is the family, which is the place where love is nurtured. More than any other institution, the Church as the Body of Christ is expected to exemplify this love, supporting families to be equally loving.

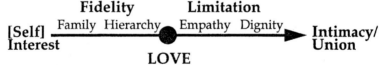

Yet [Self]Interest is often the natural consequence of being in a leadership position. The person at the top sees the whole system and has to make decisions from that standpoint while representing the system to the rest of society. It is very easy at this level to conclude that "only I" have sufficient information to make the real decisions. This is institutionalized narcissism: the leader believes that only he or she can make the decisions which everyone else should support.

The irony of this narcissism is that very frequently it is not a problem initiated by the leader, but one which he or she has inherited. It can result from the condition of the institution rather than the particular style of the leader. As an example, churches often impose unrealistic expectations of moral, pastoral and administrative perfection upon their ministers. These expectations then are often converted into a dependence that gives ministers total control or power over decisions affecting the life of their congregations. Consequently, the minister is unable to find peers within the congregation and eventually becomes a victim of role and circumstance. This is particularly reinforced when the leader receives additional benefits and a much higher salary than his or her staff.

Here we see that, obedience to the leader is going to require a hierarchical structure within the organization. One positive reason for hierarchy is its efficiency when one has limited, skilled resources. When there is an emergency, or when there is a lot of pressure for quick results, this model is the most efficient. Hierarchy, however, necessarily reinforces competition.

When the mature person is seized by the vision of intimacy and union, the problems of competition can be overcome. Hierarchy becomes Empathy, which, in a corporate or community situation means the ability to delegate authority. A new level of trust is discovered as the leader shares and listens more deeply. Empathy implies time is taken to exercise Human Dignity, which leads to a deeper sharing. At the institutional level, when Listening and Sharing facilitate delegation, all persons involved in the interaction are dignified.

While intimacy and union are individual states of growth, there is, an institutional connection. At the highest level, intimacy in the institutional setting is the creation of interdependent administrative communities in which total delegation is possible. In the faith community this is exemplified by Jesus and the twelve apostles.

Evil and Love: Forces in Conflict

Of particular significance to the disciple is the way the three paths connect to form conflicting forces in our lives for good or for evil. Each of us grows through institutional influences -- our family, then school and finally the place where we find our ministry. We are persons in systems -- that is we influence and are continually influenced by each of the institutional systems of which we are a part. In a creative situation, there is motion backward and forward between our influence on a system and its influence on us. Many people feel powerless in a system and often a little afraid of what may happen if they question authority. They have good reason, for the most powerfully frightening experience of evil is a system experience. Let us look at how this occurs.

The Forces of Evil

Each of us experiences a constant tension between the negative and positive ends in each of the paths. Although [Self]Preservation, Security and [Self]Interest are not always bad in themselves, our most destructive side is likely to emerge when these become our primary concerns. When this occurs, the phenomenon of evil can take over a person, especially someone in a leadership position. This state is called "possession" and it is always a system phenomenon.

This is best illustrated with a concrete example from the congregation where I was an assistant minister. John was a member of the church board and had become stressed and moody. One day his wife came to see me and asked if I would talk to him.

John and his family had been members of the local church for twenty years. For about fifteen years, John had owned a printing business around the corner from the church. He employed ten people. Over the last five years much of the local industry had relocated to another area, and John's business declined rapidly. He liked the area near the church, and he did not want to relocate. When his wife complained that he was hardly at home, he replied that if he did not work during the evening he might miss some customers. He noted, "In order to survive I must work harder and produce more." The spiral down is always started when the [Self] Preservation button is pushed.

As the pressure increased, John's Security decreased. Insecurity is manifested by a person becoming more anxious and more controlling. "Church is now a waste of time. He only has time for work," his wife said. John used to ask his employees for help, and he always shared the finances with them so they could plan the next month's work. One of his employees told me John watched the books everyday. "As if it makes that much difference," he added. As the pressure mounted, John's very Survival seemed at stake. Feelings of tension and insecurity about the future increased, and as a result, John took over all management and administrative control and made all the decisions. An employee who had been with him for eight years left because he was being treated like a child, and was no longer allowed to make any decisions on his own.

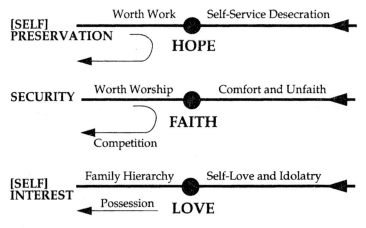

Looking at the diagram we see that John's values stay to the left of the diagram, moving from [Self]Preservation to [Self]Worth (Worth in the diagram) and then to Work. From Work to Security, passing Worship and Worth again, and down to Hierarchy and finally [Self]Interest. The tension produced its own momentum. John stated that no decisions relating to the business (his Work) could be made without his approval. Trusted employees had less and less access to him. The business became more of a hierarchy than before. Work as Efficiency and Productivity were now the exclusive values that determined whether or not a person remained with the company. Particularly disturbing was the fact that John's behavior carried over into his family life and the way he treated his friends. Finally [Self]Interest began to take over, and John now found himself watching not only everything, but everyone.

John was at the point where possession can occur, the point at which any opinion different from one's own is suspect. When a person becomes completely closed off to the opinions of others he or she cannot be reached. At its worst, possession is reinforced by drug or alcohol dependency.

Erich Fromm posits that this experience of narcissism is the borderline between sanity and insanity. He writes:

"A particular instance of narcissism which lies on the borderline between sanity and insanity can be found in some men who have reached an extraordinary degree of power. The Egyptian Pharaohs, the Roman Caesars, the Borgias, Hitler, Stalin, Trujillo -- they all show similar features. They have obtained absolute power; their word is the ultimate judgment of everything, including life and death; there seems to be no limit to their capacity to do what they want. They are gods, limited only by illness, age and death. They try to find a solution to the problem of human existence by the desperate attempt to transcend the limitation of human existence."[1]

This condition is the experience of evil we all encounter in differing degrees. It is the negative force brought about by the peculiar combination of person and system (institution); it is the condition and experience of sin that alienates us from the community, our family and finally God. Fromm's examples are people who had exceptional power. But the same experience of using power for evil can affect anyone who works and/or lives in an institution and takes ministry seriously. Temptation comes to all of us, including our Lord: "Full of the Holy Spirit, Jesus returned from the Jordan, and for forty days was led by the spirit up and down the wilderness and tempted by the devil" (Luke 4:1-2).

I am not suggesting that this is all there is to be said about evil. Not at all! My point is simply that evil occurs very often in a system or institutional setting and that it enters into individuals who influence others, spreading the misery they themselves feel. The example of John illustrates that it can happen to anyone. In fact, evil is a challenge that every disciple should expect to encounter.

The Negation of Gospel Values

The very values that were the foundation for the Gospel expression of Faith, Hope and Love become subverted into the self as possession. On the right side of the diagram you can see the consequence of this downward spiral. The consequences in the three paths are as follows.

From Hope to Hopelessness and Desecration: As John became entrapped by the compulsion for [Self] Preservation he lost his vision and hope for creative alternatives in his business. Rather than turning to his employees he went into himself. Hope became hopelessness. Rather than giving service to others, he became preoccupied with self-service.

On a grander scale, evil moves from a preoccupation with the preservation of self to a total disregard of the environment. Rather than Ecority, its opposite, desecration of the environment, is experienced. One of the worst examples in recent history was the intentional dumping of oil into the Persian Gulf during the war with Iraq.

From Faith to Unfaith: Next John became increasingly less secure and, as a consequence, more controlling. At its root this is a preoccupation with comfort, with avoidance of risk -- and is, therefore, a state of unfaith. Faith turns inward as a total reliance on oneself rather than God. It is the beginning of the experience of idolatry where only "I" can be trusted. The important thing to note is that all the other values that were a part of this continuum (right side of the diagram) such as Search, Truth and Justice are also negated. They never come to fruition because of John's obsession with self. John's family experienced this as withdrawal from them.

From Love to Possessed Love: On the third path we see love as the possibility of Intimacy withering into self-love through the experience of possession. We see the ultimate example of idolatry when the self is considered to be a little god.

The experience of possession traps John in a life-denying spiral negating positive values such as Sharing, Trust, Human Dignity and Intimacy. Gospel values have become subverted into human values as the Faith, Hope and Love elements are separated from each other, sucked into the dark hole of the possessed person. John's denial that anything is wrong is one sign of this. Others are his inability to listen to the advice of others and his need to make all critical decisions about his life no matter who else is affected.

The Forces of Love

John finally became ill with exhaustion. He was alone with his family, when a group of faithful friends from his church and his business turned up at his sick bed. We confronted him with his need to change, but we did it with love and prayer. We confronted John with the reality that he was in danger of losing not only his business, but also his family. Then he was prepared to listen. As a counselor I must note that his readiness to listen was rare, since the experience of possession is very difficult to break through. I was not able to do it alone, it took much more -- it took community. John's loving community made it possible for him to change.

As we have already discussed, when we achieve a certain point of spiritual maturity in the three paths, we are grasped by these higher values and pulled forward to higher levels of development. This is the experience of God's grace. To be grasped by these values, the element of faith must enter in. James Fenhagen writes, "To become a disciple means to see for oneself the values that energized the life of Jesus of Nazareth, to struggle with them, until there comes that moment when by the grace of God they become our own."[2]

To be grasped by such values is to experience the grace of God in our lives. Because we are created in the image of God, these values are an innate part of our nature, just as much as our need for [Self]Preservation, Security and [Self]Interest. The values that grasp us from the future, (those on the right hand of the diagram from Phase IV on the Faith Map,) are Ecority, Word and Intimacy as the need for union. Our expanded diagram now looks as follows.

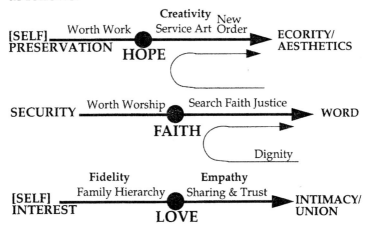

Now Love replaces narcissism and connects us with God's grace. This means we need to respond to [Self]Preservation with love rather than anxiety. At the opposite end lies Intimacy -- the solution to the problem of human and spiritual regression and increasing anxiety. Intimacy, at the human level, is the sharing of one's deepest hopes, joys, anxieties and fears with an equal who shares the same with you. It is here, as Thomas Oden points out, that an experience of transcendence occurs.

"Intimates are aware that their most significant exchanges are not merely body transactions, but as persons in encounter, or the meeting of spirit with spirit. What really happens in intimacy has to do with the spirit-spirit communion or interpersonal communion, two persons experiencing their beings poignantly united. When they are most together they are most aware of that which transcends their togetherness. Their oneness reflects a deeper capacity for coherence in the universe."[3]

This experience of union within the human experience of intimacy with another person includes revelations of even more significance. Evelyn Underhill, writing on the development of human spiritual consciousness, noted that this will for union is a gift that makes humankind capable of union with God.[4] As we study the lives of the mystics, we discover that one obvious consequence of divine union is increased capacity for intimacy with other human beings. *The very act of intimacy with God is a precondition in the disciple for the development and nurturance of the faith community. Inti-*

macy and Creativity are the essence of what it means to be human -- and the pursuit of Truth and Justice through the Word are its consequence.

As we look at the Love path, intimacy with God at the human level dignifies the human being. It is this acting out of the value of Human Dignity that leads automatically to a deeper concern -- Sharing and Listening to others. It evolves into empathic listening. At the institutional level this is expressed through a quality faith community such as John's. The honest sharing and gentle confrontation enabled John to break the narcissistic cycle which entrapped him.

As the capacity for interpersonal communion moves to deeper levels of sharing and trusting, the delegation of personal power naturally follows. This exposes us to a new freedom to be ourselves. Along with this freedom comes a renewed sense of individual limitations. When we are able to face our shortcomings and laugh about them -- and even celebrate them -- a new Independence is mobilized. This sort of independence does not easily regress to narcissism because it has emerged from its opposite, Intimacy.

As grace continues to pull us, empathetic sharing introduces new knowledge or awareness as a natural result of the interaction. The main quality required here is the continued ability to risk, to have faith in the God-given potential of others. Faith at this point implies a mutual condition of accountability and responsibility. In John's experience it was precisely this level of sharing and cooperation with his staff that eventually enabled him to get his business back on track even though it did take a different form.

The key to understanding spiritual growth is to see that it is an expansion of choices and possibilities, of greater freedom to be who we are, whereas movement towards narcissism restricts choices and the feeling of freedom. Greater interpersonal communion exposes us to the ideas of others, and as such is life-giving and energy-producing. It is precisely the feeling of having been loved (Intimacy) and the freedom to make choices that gives the human being meaning. The discovery of Meaning is actually the discovery of truth.

A concern raised at this juncture is the problem of discerning those choices and actions necessary to maximize the growth and quality of our faith community -- be it our family, our church or an administrative group to which we belong. This type of turning inward connects us to our brothers and sisters through the Body of Christ. The connection is the Holy Spirit dwelling within each of us, transcending individuality and linking "the within" of everyone, like a great net, to the faith community. The disciple creatively seeking the truth in a spirit of love is guided by the Holy Spirit. The act of prayerfully making life-giving choices in harmony with God's call for the individual and the group is the central process of spiritual guidance known as the discernment of spirits.

Finally, the movement on the second path, Faith, inspired by this need for meaning, becomes energized by a passion for Justice. The movement up, having been initiated in Intimacy and Human Dignity, is now acted out institutionally as a concern for Justice and the rights of all people. Until this point, however, the movement is related to the individual as a disciple, as he or she deals with others in an institutional setting. The upswing on the preceding diagram continues as the pursuit of truth and the need for meaning are lived out the context of vocation as Service.

This movement is the foundation of the disciple's specific ministry. Having shared and examined limitations, having risked choices and decisions in faith and having discovered and discerned truth and meaning in a "we" context through the Spirit's guidance, the disciple becomes aware of his or her unique ministry. The disciple is now certain of his or her particular vocation and sees it as a service, no matter what the job, because it lies within the greater context of God's Kingdom.

It is precisely this sense of being a part of the greater whole, of being grasped by a new awareness of the infinite order of things that draws the disciple forward. It is the experience of transcendence, which is no less than a renewed awareness of one's limitations as well as of the infinite possibilities. This infinite future is Ecority and the will within each of us to create and be co-creators with God.

As the disciple moves from Limitation and Independence to a new sense of ministry called "vocation," he or she suddenly becomes conscious in a new way of how the parts of any system or institution relate to its whole. This system awareness is the emergence of what I have called "system skills," a peculiar blend of imagination, sensitivity and competence which gives rise to the capacity to see all the parts of a system of administration as it relates to the whole. It is the ability to plan and design change in that system (institutions, societies and bodies of knowledge) so as to enhance maximum growth of the individual parts.

In this way, the disciple moves finally from ministry as Service (exercising his/her creative vocation) to the value of Construction/New Order. This is the building of the Body of Christ. Disciples at this point strive in cooperation with their co-workers to design their institutions in such a way that the resulting management structure will be the kind of community that enhances the maximum spiritual growth of each person. At the same time, in an effort to enhance societal growth as well, disciples attempt to design institutions with values in harmony with God's plan of salvation. Thus, communal development is a process of communal discernment of spirits.

At this point, due to institutional strain and the sudden increase of complexity in the disciple's life, detachment becomes essential for continued spiritual growth -- indeed to the very survival of the disciple. To remain strong at this apex of development the disciple must learn to distance from daily stress and anxiety. The practical implications of this will be the focus of the next chapter.

Conclusion

There are "faith, hope and love," said Saint Paul, "but the greatest of these is love." In the above schema, love is the starting point of spiritual growth, ideally initiated in the family as the development of interpersonal communion. It is also the origin of discipleship and ministry. Love helps us battle the destructive forces of evil.

Love's positive force is now easier to understand. The movement begins with the need for intimacy and the search for union on the path we call Love. The motivation here is the gift of love in each of us, the first manifestation of the Spirit within. This desire for love leads us to share more with others and listen attentively. We have greater appreciation for the gifts we observe in others. With the exercise of Mutual Responsibility/Accountability, new levels of communal interaction give fuller meaning as greater awareness of Human Dignity and Justice emerges. A more specific, goal-directed sense of ministry results.

At this last stage, an obvious irony exists. If the disciple is not a person of prayer striving to see and act through his or her daily union with the Lord, the pressures can become so strong that the demonic can once again take over. In other words, the great leader with great vision can easily conclude that the only way to do things is as he or she directs. The leader suddenly becomes a Hitler or a Stalin. At every level the danger exists for evil to triumph.

The specific ministry or Vocation is the call to

the disciple for creative service. The dimension of Hope is now pulling the disciple to lead, which at this point calls for prayer and detachment from the stresses of daily life as pressures and responsibilities increase. The vision of the disciple is now global, for he or she sees that the same values that once energized Jesus are now calling through the faith community. The desire for Creativity now becomes the desire to be a co-creator. Ecority exceeds personal concerns for Harmony in society and involves such concerns as building communities and institutions so that they interface with other institutions as part of the overall plan -- God's plan of history for all people. In the next and last chapter we will examine the resources that the disciple needs to maintain a quality relationship with the Lord and the faith community.

Chapter 6

The Disciple's Discipline

*When we despair of gaining inner transformation
through the human power of will and
determination, we are open to a wonderful new
realization; inner righteousness is a gift from God
to be graciously received. The needed change within
us is God's work, not ours. The demand is for an
inside job, and only God can work from the inside.
We cannot attain or earn this righteousness of the
kingdom of God; it is grace that is given.*

Richard Foster
Celebration of Discipline: The Path to Spiritual Growth

Celebration of Discipline: The Path to Spiritual Growth

This final chapter will discuss the requirements the disciple needs to sustain high levels of spiritual maturity. As we have noted thus far, the disciple always works within an institutional community. As we grow spiritually, we recognize that our lives form a battlefield between the forces of good and evil. Spiritual writers of all ages have frequently asked how we can discern and choose directions that follow the paths of Faith, Hope and Love, and confront the forces of evil. How do we live our lives in accordance with God's plans for us?

The call to discipleship is precisely to discern those things that will enhance the spiritual growth of all persons working in the faith community to further God's plans of salvation. For religious leaders, this is difficult because most of those they work with are volunteers. For the disciple ministering in a secular institution, this is difficult because he or she must allow change to occur within narrow limits and goals set by the secular world. Both jobs are stressful and both need extensive support if evil is to be thwarted.

To discern spirits we must continually develop our own spiritual and emotional life. We must also receive support in our continued spiritual development from our primary faith community. We must intentionally plan strategies for spiritual growth. These strategies or resources are the subject matter of this final chapter. I have divided the chapter into two parts. The first part deals with personal spiritual resources for faith development, and the second discusses the communal resources necessary for our ministry.

PERSONAL SPIRITUAL RESOURCES

The most personal experience of God for the Christian is in the person of Jesus of Nazareth. He is an experience of the ultimate gift of grace, as well as the embodiment of the values and priorities that God wishes us to live out in our covenant relationship to God. Theology helps us clarify our definition of covenant as well as our understanding of Jesus as gift and what that means to us in our response of faith.

Our relationship with Jesus gives us the possibility of salvation. Just as Jesus cared for the poor and the abandoned, healed the sick and confronted the injustices of this world, so we as disciples are called to be energized by the same values. If we agree to this, we are promised support, forgiveness when we "foul things up" and new life. This new life, the experience of resurrection after death, gives our lives meaning, creativity and love every time we risk for others.

Resource 1: Knowledge of Faith

Right faith is the first and most essential condition of spiritual growth. Faith is our own personal response to our experience of God. More than an intellectual pursuit, faith must be tempered by experience. The basis for our faith is regular study of the Bible. A first critical resource, therefore, is a good modern translation of a Bible. I recommend an annotated reference Bible. There are many excellent translations today including, *The New Revised Standard Version*, *The New English Bible* and *The New Jerusalem Bible*. Two helpful reference works are *The Interpreter's Bible* (a twelve-volume commentary) and *The Interpreter's Dictionary of the Bible* (a four-volume illustrated encyclopedia). As we study the Bible and the ways in which men and women of long ago experienced God, we learn more about the meaning of our faith. The study of biblical theology is, therefore, essential to our spiritual journey. We cannot be energized by Gospel values if we do not understand the Gospel. Our faith, is our most fundamental resource. Daily scriptural reading is not only an intellectual pursuit but also an experience of the death-resurrection cycle. The Psalms, the Old and New Testaments, especially the Gospels, are a constant reliving of the cycle of life, death and resurrection. When read, the accounts connect with the archetypes in each of us, aiding our personal spiritual journeys.

In *Stages of Faith* James Fowler notes that a person's faith stance changes depending on his/her level of spiritual maturity. Fowler asserts that everyone, even the atheist, has a faith stance. He shows that when we talk to others, we do so through the screen of our faith and value stance. For example, if I base my faith on the value of [Self] Preservation --"looking after number one"-- then my attitude toward others is going to be guarded at best. This distrust and disdain of other people will prevent me from learning from them. However, if my faith stance is Christian and I believe in viewing all human beings as children of God, my attitude will be very different and I will listen to people no matter who they are. I will see them through different eyes. Understanding our own faith and religious tradition is very important. An excellent resource in this regard is *Exploring American Religion* by Denise and John Carmody.

Resource 2: Knowledge of Self
Values and Faith Integration

Throughout this book we have been exploring values and the need for us to know our value priorities and how they direct us to what Scripture is saying to us. This resource -- knowledge of self -- recognizes that our values point to the deepest aspect of what is human in us and others. For the disciple, the values must be Gospel values. As we have seen, Gospel values are always connected by Love to Faith and Hope, the hope that we are part of the kingdom and that we are instrumental in bringing its reality into the lives of those whom we serve.

The most significant behavior for the Christian is love, the infinite respect for the value of others. This is grace in action, for it is not possible to love others unless I first recognize my own infinite value. This is an implicit truth, because God loved me first and completely. An interesting resource that connects the concept of Word and the human dimension through the resource of counseling psychology is *Words Made Flesh: Scripture, Psychology and Human Communication* by Fran Ferder. In it Ferder writes:

"The Christian Scriptures were written to keep alive the memories of Jesus and to proclaim his teachings. Their particular focus is the life and mission of Jesus. They advocate fidelity to discipleship. They address the way of Christian love, and they offer stories derived from the memories of the apostles to give Christian examples of that love."

"The science of psychology developed to better understand and explain how people act, grow and relate. Its particular focus is human behavior. It advocates good mental health. It addresses the way people behave, and it offers specific principles derived from research to guide the development of healthy interpersonal relationships."[1]

One way to know ourselves is by becoming aware of our values. By being clear about our values, we discover our most essential needs on one hand and God's call to us on the other hand. Value awareness is necessary so that the disciple can build a sound faith experience.

A key resource for discovering and exploring values, is the *The Journey of Discipleship* program. The program offers concrete tools for spiritual growth by determining what values participants hold, providing participants with individual profiles of their primary values, connecting those values with Scripture and helping participants explore these connections in a personal journal.[2]

Knowledge Integration

One of the central directives of spiritual leaders from every tradition is "know thyself." I call this knowledge integration because I believe this statement means more than simple self-awareness. I believe it means integrating the knowledge and skills necessary for personal and professional success. At the heart of knowledge integration is basic education. To survive as disciples, we must be well educated and trained in our professions. We must feel competent in what we do. If I am a religious educator, I must be a competent educator, and if I am an astronomer, I must be excellent in geometry and physics. Each of us must work hard to develop our gifts.

The good disciple today appreciates learning but also realizes that we all lack knowledge some of the time. We need to learn from experience, and also nurture our natural curiosity for new knowledge and understanding.

Resource 3: Time Management

For anyone on a spiritual pilgrimage one of the most important skills is detachment. This is the ability to separate ourselves from the pressures of the world in order to see ourselves clearly in relationship to God. Detachment is a very important step in discernment because, when we separate ourselves from daily pressures and anxieties, we are able to see ourselves objectively, and only then can we discern clearly. Time management can play an important role in this process.

What is involved here is not only the strict management of time but also the struggle to harmonize work and play. A balance of work and play is important for spiritual development.

In a monumental book called *The Shape of the Liturgy* Dom Gregory Dix writes of how the early Church and the Church of the medieval period wisely adapted a process of sanctification of time. Each part of the day was initiated with prayers of praise, thus sanctifying time. For instance, at daybreak the office of Lauds (praise) would begin and the bells would toll the start of the work day. To mark the sixth hour, at noon, the office of Sext would be said. Finally Vespers, or Evensong in Old English, would be said as the light of day faded and evening approached. For the great monasteries and cathedrals of Europe this ordering of time with parish bells and songs of praise was an attempt to build the kingdom of God on earth. More than anything else, it gave people hope and a sense of meaning amid war, squalor and disease. It helped them detach from the anxieties of the day.

The swing-shift and seven-day work week make this simple medieval formula impractical today. I suggest another approach to the ordering and sanctification of time. I first wrote about this in *Value Clarification as Learning Process: A Handbook for Religious Educators*. The plan divides the day into our activities of work, maintenance, play and high play.

Work is my basic vocation, what I do to make a living. Maintenance is what I do to maintain my body. It includes such things as sleep and personal hygiene. Since we are social beings, maintenance also includes listening to and helping other people with their problems. Work and maintenance are different in that work is a "doing" activity that may physically drain us and make us physically tired, whereas "maintenance" of other people drains significant emotional energy from us. Both are related to duty, obligation or contract.

Play is the opposite of work because it is not duty-related. There are forms of play that take as many skills as our work. I call this "high play." This form of play includes such things as intimacy and contemplation. It requires the same discipline and skills as my work, and like play it is recreative for me. The difference between work and maintenance, on the one hand, and play, on the other, is in the types of human relationships involved. We relate to a different set of people in the work place from those we enjoy playing with.

The work and maintenance sectors of daily life limit the possibilities for relationships and tend to be energy-draining. We are always bound by duty in some way when we are working or looking after (maintaining) others. Work forms the basis of our security and usually involves specific duties and obligations. If the work involves in-depth interaction with other people as discipleship does, especially in pastoral work, then it demands much maintenance of others and drains emotional and mental energy. When we enjoy our work, we tend to work long hours and are more likely to encounter problems with intimate co-workers. This may drain us even more.

As we leave our work and begin to relax, play is initiated. This is the first stage of detachment from work. When we are fully relaxed, total detachment takes over. Because play requires that we be totally ourselves, the relationships here are only with our most trusted intimates and friends, usually not co-workers. When work and play become mixed -- often the case with enthusiastic people in ministry -- the maintenance aspect increases considerably, and the play aspect diminishes.

To grow spiritually we must harmonize our time in work and play. The spiritual journey requires a balance between work and play. We must ask these discernment questions of ourselves: Am I working too many hours each week? Do I see enough of my family? Do I set aside time for quality play? These are the kinds of questions to ask before detachment to determine if detachment is being achieved. I have found the following discernment questions helpful in aiding persons who are seeking this balance in order to be detached:

Time and Work: What is the most work you can do before you compromise the highest quality possible for you? What is the most you can do before you compromise the highest qualities of those you work and play with, whether family or co-workers? (Answer with a specific number of hours.)

Time and the Work/Play Ratio: What is the minimal amount of recreation you need to forget the worries of work? (Answer with a specific amount of time per week.) What are you doing to develop recreation and high play activities?

Time and Maintenance: What amount of listening can you do, and what range of activities directed at helping others can you accept before the best you could be is compromised? (Answer with respect to activities that are most draining for you.)

Time and Maintenance/Play Ratio: What is the minimum amount of support you need from friends and those with whom you work in order to be the best person you feel you can be? (Answer in terms of specific hours and weekly activities.)[3]

Resource 4: The Body

Jesus began his ministry by fasting for forty days alone in the desert. Though he probably drank a little water, he ate nothing for the entire period. His physical condition must have been excellent for him to fast for such a long time. Following his example, an important dimension of the preparation for prayer is maintaining optimum physical health. Care must be taken to avoid excessive use of alcohol, tobacco or any chemical substances for emotional support.

Attention must be given to diet, weight and blood pressure as well as regular physical exercise. Occasionally when physical condition allows, the disciple might consider fasting. When we look and feel in good physical shape, our personal sense of worth improves and our presence with others is enhanced.

At times of stress and anxiety physical exercise can help dissipate so-called nervous energy. It can also re-energize us if we become lethargic. Special attention to diet during stress can also be restorative. Books on this topic are plentiful. Three to begin with are *The Royal Canadian Air Force Exercise Plan for Physical Fitness*, *The New Aerobics* by Kenneth Cooper and *Diet for a Small Planet* by Frances Moore Lappe.

Christ began his spiritual journey through fasting. "Then Jesus was led by the Spirit into the wilderness to be tempted by the devil. He fasted forty day and forty nights, and afterwards he was famished" (Matthew 4:1-2). Fasting has been a spiritual discipline throughout the ages. It is certainly not a discipline for everyone and must be done with overall attention to the body through diet and exercise. Fasting is total abstinence from food with constant drinking of water.

For those who want to pursue fasting a few reminders may be helpful: (1) Fasting should be undertaken only after sufficient preparation through diet and exercise. (2) Check with a medical doctor to ensure that your health is good enough to carry out such a venture. (3) Fasting should never be done alone but rather as a community experience. (4) After an extended fast, gradual assimilation of liquids is necessary for several days before solid foods can be eaten. (5) The length of the fast is determined before the fast. Fasting must end at this time and not extended by individuals who want to lose weight or do not feel hungry. To learn more about fasting, I recommend Louis Fischer's *The Life of Ghandi* and *Fasting Rediscovered: A Guide to Health and Wholeness for Your Body Spirit* by Thomas Ryan.

Resource 5: Deep Relaxation

Relaxation reduces the anxiety and tension in the body and the mind. As this happens we become more present to the moment and to those around us.

Anxiety is worry about the future that is conditioned by the past. Memories of past failure or guilt are transferred into the future. When these memories are felt in the present we experience tension and frustration. For example, if I forgot an appointment this morning and feel guilty about not remembering, I may become anxious about the outcome and about the anger of the person I let down. This makes me tense. When I relax, the present and past disappear and with them the tension. Detachment and meditation exercises (see Resource 6) help us forget and separate ourselves from these daily tensions.

The purpose of deep relaxation is heightened attention to the present moment. This enables us to detach from worry, and in doing so we become aware of the presence of God. The first step in relaxing for meditation is proper body posture. Any posture will do as long as the spine is straight and erect. After assuming an appropriate posture, the relaxation exercises begin. There are many standard methods involving tightening and relaxing the muscles, breathing exercises, imagining various parts of the body and concentrating on relaxation response sentences.

A very helpful volume for both body posture and relaxation for meditation is *Meditation in Depth* by Klemens Tilmann. Also see William Johnston's *Silent Music: The Science of Meditation* and Herbert Benson's *The Relaxation Response*.

Resource 6: Meditation

Meditation is the period of waiting that follows Scripture reading or relaxation -- waiting in silence for God to speak. There are two parts to the waiting experience, which together make up the practice of meditation: detachment and contemplation.

First begin with the practice of detachment or "non-attachment" as it is termed in the East. A western psychologist and the founder of psychosynthesis, Roberto Assagioli, developed this to a fine art. His term for non-attachment is disidentification. Basically it is a method and technique for separating ourselves from stress, anxieties and thoughts that distract us from being present with ourselves and God. These exercises, which are an extension of relaxation methods, enable us to detach ourselves from specific habits or concerns that may be troubling. This approach is the basis for most methods of meditation.

Contemplation follows detachment. There are different methods of contemplation. One method involves passive concentration keeping the mind blank by repetition of a mantra -- a single sound, word or phrase. Another method uses images and imaging which take the mind on patterned inner journeys. Although there are many methods of contemplation, the intention is always the same: centeredness, deep concentration and attention to the present. The purpose is to be fully in the present moment waiting for God to speak.

Some resources for methods of detachment are *The Way of Non-Attachment,* by Dhiravamsa, published by Turnstone Press of London, and *Psychosynthesis: A Manual of Principles and Techniques* by Roberto Assagioli, published by Hobbs, Dorman and Company.

Resources dealing extensively with contemplation and meditation are *The Open Way* by Gerald May and *Living Simply Through the Day: Spiritual Survival in a Complex Age* by Tilden Edwards. Both are published by Paulist Press. *The Kingdom Within* by John Sanford and *The Other Side of Silence* by Morton Kelsey use the image approach and add the dimension of dream interpretation as a source of inner wisdom.

So far all the resources have stressed the preparation of the disciple for the spiritual battle. They help strengthen the life of the body, mind and spirit of the disciple as an individual. However, these resources are insufficient on their own. As a member of the Body of Christ, the disciple must also have support from the faith community which brings with it its own needs and resources.

COMMUNAL RESOURCES

Just as it is necessary for an individual to have the right faith orientation, so the disciple must also have a right institutional faith, an understanding of what Saint Paul called the Body of Christ: "Just as each of our bodies has separate parts and each part has a separate function, so all of us in union with Christ form one body, and as parts of it we belong to each other. Our gifts differ according to the grace given us" (Romans 12:4-6).

For Paul, the Spirit of Christ in each believer unites all believers in a cohesive organism he calls the Body. Each of us forms an interdependent whole with each other. Leaders cannot function without followers; both need each other. Each person's gifts and ministry are indispensable to the whole. Paul saw the person as a part of a system.

Gerald May points out in his book *Pilgrimage Home*, "There are some aspects of spiritual growth which require totally private self-confrontation, and there are aspects which are so numinous that they cannot be communicated. Both of these factors make aloneness a very real and legitimate dimension of the spiritual search. Yet at the same time, there is real help from other human beings. The support of others, their critique, guidance and their historical heritage are not always available in one form or another, but they are absolutely necessary."[4]

In the faith community we gather, each with a separate spiritual struggle and witness together in hearing the Word and in breaking the bread that we are one in the Lord. We may not feel one in the Lord or resurrected, but we are in fact a community of support. This reality, stated weekly, asserts what is needed for us to remain spiritually whole without being compromised. This is particularly true of the disciple who is in a position of leadership with significant influence over other lives.

To sustain high levels of leadership and spiritual integrity under pressure, each person needs three additional sources of support:

- an intimacy system
- a work delegation and support system
- a peer support system.

From my own observations, when more than one of these sources is absent, the stress on a leader with considerable responsibility is very high. The less pressure from the system, the fewer supports required. To view this more clearly, let us first examine each resource separately.

Resource 7: The Intimacy System

Persons in leadership positions (and anyone who wishes to grow spiritually) must share intimately with at least one other person on a regular basis. In an intimate relationship, there need not be a physical dimension but simply an experience of deep sharing. Intimacy implies regular sharing of all my fears and hopes openly with another person who shares equally with me. It is not counseling or spiritual direction as much as sharing with a peer.

Why is such a relationship necessary? As each of us grows in spiritual maturity and becomes more involved in our service to others, we need to see ourselves as others see us. This is perhaps the most important step in reaching maturity. Part of growing spiritually is the ability to integrate our inner perceptions of ourselves with the impressions we give to others. Only deep and honest sharing allows others to see us clearly. This kind of sharing, is only helpful when it is done regularly and consistently in an intentional way. Intimacy requires nurturance between two persons over a long period of time; it is growth in mutual trust and radical commitment to loyalty and confidentiality. Although this is the ideal of marriage, it does not automatically occur. Couples must work very hard to see that it in fact happens.

Since intimacy is a need each of us has, and since it is also a requirement for spiritual growth, it presents a problem for many people in leadership positions because it involves the risk of vulnerability. Yet when I risk intimacy with another, I develop a much deeper and more expansive view of human relationships. Persons who are single and those with weak marriages have legitimate fears about becoming vulnerable, but whatever the extenuating circumstances, intimate sharing is essential for spiritual growth.

The intimate relationship -- as a spiritual necessity -- cannot be with a co-worker, since this too often confuses authority, power and duty with deep sharing. It often will not occur unless the institution, whether family or community, encourages intimacy and sees it as valuable.

130

I have worked with many religious congregations that discouraged any close relationships in or
out of the system. Often the superior general of
such a community becomes isolated and lonely because of his or her authority, yet unable to consult
with other superiors outside the congregation.
Open and healthy intimacy, therefore, needs to be
understood as one of the essential components of
spiritual growth for discipleship. Intimacy is a sign
of higher levels of spiritual and leadership functions.

Resource 8: Work Delegation and Support

Unlike the intimacy system, this resource involves the development of a support community
with the people at work. There are two prerequi-
sites for such a community: an understanding that
anything we do can, if necessary, be delegated for a
limited period of time and our work team must be
comprised of supportive peers.

The first condition refers to the fact that such a
community cannot exist without support from the
institution. For me to delegate all I do, the people I
work with must have just as many skills and as
much authority as I have.   An individual may not
have this, but a team will. Without delegation, total
detachment from work, even when the leader is
tired and exhausted, is not possible.

The second prerequisite is the necessity for a
support community of peers to allow optimum
working conditions. Peers are chosen equals who
are more skilled and competent in certain areas

than I am, and to whom I am willing to delegate. But an individual disciple or leader cannot bring about these conditions alone. They come about through the enthusiasm of the leader and institutional reinforcement. Both leader and institution must work in harmony. The institution provides the financial and spiritual resources, and the leader must be mature enough to risk delegation for a higher vision.

Collegial leadership is essential for individual and institutional growth beyond a certain point. It involves not only a constant struggle against bigotry and fear of losing one's authority but also training new people, examining personal limitations and risking institutional disapproval. This work delegation and support system does not come naturally; it must be planned. The leader must initiate it by example, encouraging it in others until it becomes an acceptable part of the leadership role and function.

Resource 9: Peer Support System

The peer support system is a group of people at my professional level who are not a part of my work team but with whom I meet regularly to share ideas and receive feedback. The peer support system is intentionally organized, and individuals are paired with other individuals. It is not something done casually at annual professional conferences. It is a system of pairing with a wise partner. In his discussion of peer consultation, G. Caplan says, "Peer consultation is a process of borrowing and lending. From this process of interchange of ideas, abilities, knowledge, conceptualizing skills and workable schemes comes a mutual enrichment which enables both parties to face their respective tasks with increased enthusiasm."[5] The people involved are neither one's intimate friends nor co-workers, but a different person or group of people from whom I can receive wise feedback about work or play relationships without threat.

In this chapter, I have suggested nine resources necessary for personal and spiritual growth. They are simply a beginning list of minimum requirements for the spiritual growth of the disciple. The support groupings and relationships suggested in this last chapter are not definitive by any means. We have our friends, our solitude, our co-workers, those we trust as peer consultants, and if we are lucky, someone with whom we are intimate.

Conclusion

Values -- together with Scripture reading -- provide the spiritual connections necessary for discipleship. The goal of discipleship is intimacy with our Lord joined by the Holy Spirit through a common mission with other members in the body of Christ. Contemporary discipleship involves union with the Divine Creator, Redeemer and Sanctifier in order to fulfill the mission begun by the first disciples so many centuries ago -- the realization of God's kingdom on earth.

AFTERWORD

If you want to learn more about your own unique gifts and how to use them to advance God's kingdom on earth, then you may be interested in *The Journey of Discipleship*. This three-step program is based on the values theory in *Spiritual Connections: The Journey of Discipleship and Christian Values* and the *Hall-Tonna Inventory of Values*. The Hall-Tonna is the only instrument which measures a person's values and is the result of twenty years of research into values development by Benjamin Tonna, Lic.D. of Malta and myself.

The Three Steps

The Journey of Discipleship Questionnaire: This questionnaire is designed to gather information about your values. The 125 multiple-choice questions relate to the 125 values.

The Journey of Discipleship Profile: This profile is a four-page, computer-generated analysis of the questionnaire. It is completely confidential and can be understood only by the person who completes the questionnaire. The profile provides information for a person's faith journey, including insight into foundation, focus and future values.

The Journey of Discipleship Workbook and Manual: These materials help the individual interpret the profile and serve as information resources to extend the usefulness of the profile. Scripture references for personal reflection are included.

The materials are designed for use by individuals. However, this three-step program can be adapted for work with couples or groups. It can also serve as the basis for retreats, leadership workshops and educational series.

For more information about *The Journey of Discipleship*, write: Values Technology Inc., 532 Stonehaven Rd., Kettering, Ohio 45429; or call (513) 298-7783.

ENDNOTES

CHAPTER 1
The Spiritual Connection: Discipleship and God's Word

EPIGRAPH: Dietrich Bonhoeffer, *The Cost of Discipleship*, p. 64.

1. I no longer have this book, nor do I know if it is still in print. The author was Arthur Mee, and the book was published about 1940.

2. Merle Jordan, *Taking on the Gods*.

3. There are a number of books that refer to the relationship between the mind and the internal imaging process. Two that I particularly recommend are: James Ashbrook, *The Human Mind and the God's Mind* and John Sanford, *The Kingdom Within*.

4. See appendix. Also see, Brian P. Hall, *The Genesis Effect*.

CHAPTER 2
Values, Signs and God's Word

EPIGRAPH: Richard H. Neibuhr, *Christ and Culture*, 14-15.

1. At the time I was a student of Dr. Alfaro Sotela, a Christian psychiatrist, and Paola Friere. Central to our work was the theory that if we listened at length and with great depth we would be able to pick out critical, emotionally laden words which would point to the heart of concerns and issues held by a person or a community.

2. These 125 values, found in the appendix, resulted from research I began in 1979 with Dr. Benjamin Tonna of Malta. Our comprehensive approach to value identification, assessment and measurement is known as the *Hall-Tonna Inventory of Values*.

3. Rath, Harmin and Simon, *Values and Teaching*, 6.

4. A more detailed, personalized method of looking at values is offered through *The Journey of Discipleship*. This program provides extensive, confidential information on your value priorities that results from a computer analysis of a

questionnaire. It also includes a workbook and manual for private reflection. For more information, contact Values Technology, Inc., 532 Stonehaven Rd., Dayton, Ohio 45429.

CHAPTER 3
Faith, Hope and Love: Gospel Values as Gifts

1. Neibuhr, chapter 1, provides a discussion of hope and its relationship to eschatology in the life of Jesus.

2. Dodd, *The Epistle of St. Paul to the Romans*, 15.

3. Ibid., 17.

4. Frankl, *Man's Search for Meaning*, 154.

5. Fromm, *The Heart of Man*, 86.

6. Underhill, *Mysticism*, 24.

CHAPTER 4
Paths on the Faith Journey: Discerning God's Call

1. The values noted here are from the 125 Values found in the Appendix. Not all 125 are listed for reasons of brevity. This is a shorter list utilizing those values that are discussed in the text. For more detailed discussion see Hall, *The Genesis Effect*.

2. For example, women in Phase I tend to prioritize Wonder/Awe/Fate while men prioritize [Self] Preservation. Hence, women tend to approach the world from the depths of their inner being, and men tend to tackle the external world first by organizing and ordering it. Thus, in Phase I women and men approach the world in two different but equally valuable ways. The real differences as a consequence emerge in Phase II.

3. For more information, contact Values Technology, Inc., 532 Stonehaven Rd., Dayton, Ohio 45429.

CHAPTER 5
The Disciple's Struggle with Good and Evil

1. Fromm, *The Heart of Man*, 76-77.

2.Fenhagen, *Mutual Ministry*, 49.

3.Ogden, *Game Free*, 23.

4. Underhill, *Mysticism*.

CHAPTER 6
The Disciple's Discipline

EPIGRAPH: Foster, *Celebration of Discipline*, 5.

1. Ferder, *Words Made Flesh*, 14.

2. For more information, contact Values Technology, Inc., 532 Stonehaven Rd., Dayton, Ohio 45429.

3. A simple tool to measure time differences is available from Values Technology, Inc., 532 Stonehaven Rd., Dayton, Ohio 45429. For a more detailed discussion of time management, see Hall, *The Genesis Effect*.

4. May, *The Pilgrimage Home*, 27.

5.Caplan, ed., *Support Systems*, 270.

BIBLIOGRAPHY

Ashbrook, James B. *The Human Mind and the God's Mind*. New York: University Press of America. 1984.

Assagioli, Roberto, M.D. *The Act of the Will*. New York: Penguin Books, 1974.

Assagioli, Roberto, M.D. *Psychosynthesis: A Manual of Principles and Techniques*. New York: Hobbs, Dorman and Company, Inc., 1965.

Au, Wilkie. *By Way of the Heart: Towards a Holistic Christian Spirituality*. New York: Paulist Press, 1989.

Baillie, John. A Diary of Reading. Nashville, Tenn: Abingdon Press, 1955.

Benson, Herbert. *The Relaxation Response*. New York: William Morrow and Company, Inc., 1975.

Boff, Leonardo. Liberating Grace. New York: Orbis Books, 1979.

Bonaventure. *The Soul's Journey Into God, The Tree of Life, The Life of St. Francis*. Translated by Ewert Cousins. New York: Paulist Press, 1978.

Bonhoeffer, Dietrich. *The Cost of Discipleship. New York: Collier Books, 1963.*

Brown, Barbara B. *Stress and the Art of Biofeedback*. New York: Bantam Books, 1977.

Caplan, G. and M. Killilea, eds. *Support and Mutual Help*. New York: Grune and Straton, 1972.

Caplan, Ruth B. *Helping the Helpers to Help: Mental Health Consultation to Aid Clergymen in Pastoral Work*. New York: Seabury Press, 1972.

Carmody, Denis Lardner and John Tully Carmody. *Exploring American Religion*. Mountain View, California: Mayfield Publishing Company, 1990.

Clark, Walter Houston. *The Psychology of Religion*. New York: The Macmillan Company, 1958.

Cooper, Kenneth H. *The New Aerobics*. New York: Bantam

Books, 1970.

Corrigan, Gregory M. *Disciple Story*. Notre Dame: Ave Maria
Press, 1989.

Dhiravamsa. *The Way of Non-Attachment: The Practice of Insight
Meditation*. London: Turnstone Books, 1975.

Dodd, C.H. The Epistle of St. Paul to the Romans. London:
Hodder and Stoughton, 1960.

Dykstra, Craig and Sharon Parks. *Faith Development and
Fowler*. Birmingham: Religious Education Press, 1986.

Dix, Dom Gregory. *The Shape of Liturgy*. London: Dacre Press,
1945.

Edwards, Tilden. *Living Simply Through the Day: Spiritual
Survival in a Complex Age*. New York: Paulist Press,
1979.

Erikson, Erik H. "Identity and the Life Cycle." *Psychological
Issues*, 1 no. 1 (1959).

Fenhagen, James C. *Mutual Ministry: New Vitality for the Local
Church*. New York: Seabury Press, 1977.

Freder, Fran. Words *Made Flesh: Scripture, Psychology and
Human Communication*. Notre Dame: Ave Maria Press,
1988.

Fischer, Louis. *The Life of Mahatma Gandhi*. New York: Harper
and Brothers, 1950.

Foster Richard. *Celebration of Discipline: The Path to Spiritual
Growth*. New York: Harper and Row, 1978.

Fowler, James and Sam Keen. *Life Maps: Conversations on the
Journey of Faith*. Edited by Jerome Berryman. Waco,
Texas: Word Books, 1978.

Fowler, James. *Stages of Faith: The Psychology of Human
Development and the Quest for Meaning*. San Francisco:
Harper and Row, 1981.

Frankl, Viktor E. *Man's Search for Meaning*. New York:
Washington Square Press, Inc., 1963.

Fromm, Erich. *The Heart of Man*. New York: Perennial Library,
1964.

Greenleaf, Robert K. *Servant Leadership: A Journey into the
Nature of Legitimate Power and Greatness*. New York:
Paulist Press, 1977.

Hall, Brian P. *Value Clarification as Learning Process: A
Handbook for Religious Educators*. New York: Paulist

Press, 1973.

Hall, Brian P. *The Genesis Effect: Personal and Organizational Transformations.* New York: Paulist Press, 1986.

Hall, Brian P. *The Personal Discernment Inventory.* New York: Paulist Press, 1973.

Hall, Brian P. *Shepherds and Lovers: A Guide to Spiritual Leadership and Christian Ministry.* New York: Paulist Press, 1982.

Illich, Ivan. *Deschooling Society.* Edited by Nanda Anshen. New York: Harper and Row, 1970.

Illich, Ivan. *Toward a History of Need.* New York: Pantheon Books, 1978.

Inge, W. R. *Personal Religion and the Life of Devotion.* London: Longmans Green and Company, Ltd., 1924.

James, William. *The Varieties of Religious Experience.* New York: Collier Books, 1961.

Jaynes, Julian. *The Origin of Consciousness in the Breakdown of the Bicameral Mind.* Boston: Houghton Mifflin Company, 1976.

Johnston, William. *Silent Music: The Science of Meditation.* New York: Harper & Row, 1974.

Jordan Merle R. *Taking on the Gods.* Nashville: Abingdon Press, 1986.

Kelsey, Morton T. *The Other Side of Silence: A Guide to Christian Meditation.* New York: Paulist Press, 1976.

Kropf, Richard W. *Faith, Security and Risk: The Dynamics of Spiritual Growth.* New York: Paulist Press, 1990.

May, Gerald G. *Pilgrimage Home: The Conduct of Contemplative Practice in Groups.* New York: Paulist Press, 1979.

May, Gerald G. *The Open Way: A Meditation Handbook.* New York: Paulist Press, 1977.

Niebuhr, Richard H. *Christ and Culture Harper.* New York: Torchbooks, 1951.

Oden, Thomas C. *Game Free: A Guide to the Meaning of Intimacy.* New York: Harper and Row, 1974.

Peck, M. Scott. *The Different Drum: Community Making and Peace.* New York: Touchstone Books, 1987.

Peck, M. Scott. *The People of the Lie: The Hope for Healing Human Evil.* New York: Touchstone Books, 1983.

Peck, M. Scott. *The Road Less Travelled: A New Psychology of Love, Traditional Values and Spiritual Hope*. New York: Simon and Schuster, 1978.

Progoff, Ira. *The Practice of Process Meditation: The Intensive Journal Way to Spiritual Experience*. New York: Dialogue House Library, 1980.

Rath, Louis E., Merrill Harmin and Sidney B. Simon. *Values and Teaching: Working with Values in the Classroom*. Columbus, Ohio: Charles E. Merrill Publishing Co., 1966.

Rogers, Carl R. and William Coulson, eds. *Freedom to Learn*. Columbus, Ohio: Charles E. Merrill Publishing Company, 1969.

The Royal Canadian Air Force Exercise Plans for Physical Fitness. New York: Pocket Books, 1972.

Ryan, Thomas, CSP. *Fasting Rediscovered: A Guide to Health and Wholeness*. New York: Paulist Press, 1981.

Sanford, John A. *The Kingdom Within*. New York: Paulist Press, 1970.

Schultz, J. H., M. D. and W. Luthe, M.D. *Autogenic Methods*. Vol. 1. Edited by Wolfgang Luthe. New York: Grune and Stratton, 1969.

Schumacher, E. F. *A Guide for the Perplexed*. New York: Harper and Row, 1977.

Schweitzer, Albert. *Memories of Childhood and Youth*. New York: Macmillan, 1925.

Stern, Aaron. *Me: The Narcissistic American*. New York: Balline Books, 1979.

Stevens, Edward. *Business Ethics*. New York: Paulist Press, 1979.

Storr, Anthony. *Solitude to the Self*. New York: Ballantine Books, 1988.

Tillich, Paul. *The Courage to Be*. New Haven: Yale University Press, 1952.

Tillich, Paul. *Systematic Theology: Three Volumes in One*. Chicago: The University of Chicago Press, 1963.

Tilmann, Klemens. *Meditation in Depth: A Practical Guide to Meditation for Groups and Individuals*. New York: Paulist Press, 1979.

Tonna, Benjamin. *Gospel for the Cities: A Socio-Theology of Urban*

144

Ministry. Translated by William E. Jerman. New York: Orbis Books, 1982.

Underhill, Evelyn. *Mysticism: A Study in the Nature and Development of Man's Spiritual Consciousness.* New York: Meridian Books, 1955.

APPENDIX:
VALUES AS SIGNS OF GODS WORD

This appendix contains definitions of the 125 values that have been identified in values research. The values are listed in alphabetical order. Following each value definition are Bible verses that may reveal how the value can reflect and communicate God's Word to you.

To reflect on Scripture, first quiet your mind using some type of centering exercise such as focused breathing or the use of mantra. Then simply read the passage through in its entirety. Slowly read it a second time being very mindful of any word phrase that stirs something deep within you. Stop reading and sit quietly with the word or phrase and listen to what it tells you about your life.

Afterwards you may want to share this with a trusted friend or write it in your journal, reflecting on the following questions.

What does this reading tell me about who God is to me? What does it tell me about who I am to God? Does this passage give me clues about what God is asking me to do or to be?

Careful reflection on the Scriptures relating to your values can reveal the gifts that God is asking you to share in the shaping of God's kingdom on earth.

DEFINITIONS

1. **Accountability/Ethics:** the ability that flows from personal awareness of one's own system of moral principles
   to enrich others by addressing their conduct in relationship to their value system. This assumes the capacity to understand another's level of ethical
   maturity.
   Matt. chapters 5-7; especially 5:1-12 and 19:19; Ex.
   20:12-16; and Deut. 5:16-20. (See also Law/Rule;
   Law/Guide; Duty/Obligation; Obedience/Duty;
   Obedience/Mutual Accountability; Responsibility;
   and Mutual Responsibility/Accountability.)

2. **Achievement/Success:** accomplishing something note-
   worthy and admirable in the world of work or education.
   2 Chron. 20:20-21; Job, especially 36 and 42; Ps. 16;
   Jas. 1:22-25. (See also Economics/Profit and Econom-
   ics/Success.)

3. **Adaptability/Flexibility:** the ability to adjust oneself readi-
   ly to changing conditions and to remain pliable during ongoing processes. The concept of an open heart
   rather than a hardened heart is central to the value of
   being flexible and adaptable.
   Luke 8:2-15; Prov. 23:15-25; Matt. 5:4.

4. **Administration/Control:** having the authority to be in
   command, to exercise specific management functions
   and tasks in a business or institution, e.g. financial
   control, production planning, etc. From the Latin, administration implies "ministry or ministering to."
   1 Cor. 12:12-30; Rom. 12:1-13; Eph. 4:7-16. (See also
   Service/Vocation; Work/Labor; Corporation/New
   Order.

5. **Affection/Physical:** physical touching which expresses
   fondness or devotion. This is the concept of the body
   as a holy vessel of God's creation and applies to self-

care as well as treatment of others.
Rom. 12:1-12; 1 Cor. 6:12-20; Eph. 5:28-33.

6. **Art/Beauty/as Pure Value:** experiencing and/or providing intense pleasure through that which is aesthetically appealing in both natural and person-made creations simply for the mental and emotional stimulation and the pleasure it provides. This is the concept of the created order as good in itself.
Gen. 1; Ps. 29:1-2; Eccl. 3:1-2; Rom. 8:18-27.

7. **[Self]Assertion/Directedness:** the will to put oneself forward boldly regarding a personal line of thought or action. This values is also a dimensions of the ability to discern spirits.
Deut. 30:5-20; Prov. 3:1-8 and 16:9; 2; Thess. 3:5; 1 Cor. 12:10; Heb. 4:12-13.

8. **Being Liked:** to experience friendly feelings from one's peers.
Prov. 17:17 and 27:6; John 3:16; Eph. 4:1-6. (See also [Self] Worth and Friendship/Belonging.)

9. **Being Self:** the capacity to own the truth about oneself and the world with objective awareness of personal strengths and limitations plus the ability to act both independently and cooperatively when appropriate.
Eph. 3:4-21 and 4:9-16; Rom. 6:1-14; 2 Cor. 5:16-19; Col. 3:10; Phil. 2:8-16; 1 Tim. 4:12; 2 Tim. 1:5-7. (See also [Self] Worth; [Self]Competence/Confidence; Life/[Self] Actualization.)

10. **Care/Nurture:** to be physically and emotionally supported by family and friends throughout one's life and to value doing the same for others. The concept is that we should care for ourselves and others as God cares for us.
Matt. 6:4-34; Gal. 5:13-26; Eph. 4:1-8.

11. **Collaboration/Subsidiarity:** the ability of an organizational leader to cooperate interdependently with all levels of management to ensure full and appropriate delegation of responsibility. In Christianity this is analogous to the Body of Christ.
Rom. 12:4-9; 1 Cor. 12:4-30. (See also Service/Vocation.)

12. **Communication/Information:** effective and efficient transmission and flow of ideas and factual data within and between persons, departments and divisions of an organization.

    Heb. 13:16; Eph. 4:29-32.

13. **Community/Personalist:** sufficient depth and quality of commitment to a group, its members and its purpose so that both independent creativity and interdependent cooperation are maximized simultaneously. The modern idea and experience of community grow from the understanding of community in the early Church where the highest ideal was rooted in the concept of the Body of Christ as an interdependent unifying and loving force in society.

    1 Cor. 12:4-30; Eph. 4:1-8.

14. **Community/Supportive:** the recognition and will to create a group of peers for the purpose of ongoing mutual support and creative enhancement of each individual. The additional awareness of the need for such a group in the work environment and with peer professionals to enable detachment from external pressures that deter one from acting with clarity on chosen values and ethical principles that might be otherwise compromised.

    This value emerges from the understanding of community in the early Church which was based on the equal sharing of goods and property.

    Understanding this ideal in the context of modern culture enriches the meaning of our experience of community as supportive.

    Eph. 4:1-16; Acts 2:44-45; 4:32-5:10. (See also Accountability/Ethics and Collaboration/Subsidiarity.)

15. **[Self]Competence/Confidence:** realistic and objective confidence that one has the skill to achieve in the world of work and to feel that those skills are a positive contribution. (In the Christian context skills are termed "gifts.") This value hinges on prior development of [Self] Worth and is moving toward development of Life/Self Actualization and Being Self.

    Heb. 10:35-39; Acts. 2:38-40; 1 Cor. 12:4-11, 27-31; 1 Tim. 2:1-7; 2 Tim 2:15.

16. **Competition:** energy derived from a sense of rivalry, to be first or most respected in a given arena, e.g. sports, education or work. Ideally, Christians compete in the sense of developing their gifts to the highest level in order to bring about God's Kingdom.

    1 Cor. 9: 24-27; Heb. 12:1-4.

17. **Congruence:** the capacity to experience and express one's feelings and thoughts in such a way that what one experiences internally and communicates externally to others is the same. This value stands at the heart of personal integrity and honesty.

    Ps. 15; Ps. 51:6; John 8:32. (See also Personal/Authority/Honesty; Integration/Wholeness; and Being Self.)

18. **Construction/New Order:** the ability to develop and initiate a new institution for the purpose of creatively enhancing society. This assumes technological, interpersonal and management skills. Inherent in this value is the concept of the Kingdom of God on earth. In Genesis the concept that human beings are to be responsible for the earth develops into the concept that a new order of creation is being born.

    Gen. 1:26-30; Is. 2:6-9 and 65:17-25; Mark 1: 14; Matt. 10:2-16 and 16:13-20; Luke 6: 13-16 and 9:57-10:20; Rom. 8: 18-23; Eph. 4:1-7, 10-16.

19. **Contemplation/Asceticism**: self- discipline and the art of meditative prayer that prepares one for intimacy with others and unity with the universal order. The basic concept of Christian contemplation is that God's indwelling presence is available to each of us.

    John 15-17; Matt.6:5-18 and 14:22-23; Rom. 8:26-27.

20. **Control/Order/Discipline**: providing restraint and direction to achieve methodological arrangements of persons or things according to the prescribed rules. In Christian terms this value relates to the discipline of prayer and spiritual, emotional and educational development.

    Deut. 6:20-25; 1 Cor. 9:24-27; Eph. 6:4. (See also Education/Certification; Worship/Faith/Creed; Integration/ Wholeness; Contemplation/Asceticism.)

21. **Convivial Technology:** the capacity to apply technological expertise creatively, both organizationally and

with technical instruments, to develop means to improve social conditions in the world by improving means of distributing the basic necessities of life. This value emerges from our technological age. However it is anticipated in the scriptural concept of the dawning of a new and just age.

Gen. 1:26-31; Rev. 21.

22. **Cooperation/Complementarity:** the capacity to enable persons in a corporation or institution to work cooperatively with one another such that the unique skills and qualities of one individual supplement, support and enhance the skills and qualities of the others in the group.

Rom. 12: 4-9; 1 Cor. 12:4-30. (See also Service/Vocation and Collaboration/Subsidiarity.)

23. **Corporation/New Order:** the skills, capacity and will to create new organizational styles or to improve present institutional forms in order to creatively enhance society. The best models are found in the beginnings of the Church.

Matt. 10:2-16 and 16: 13-20; Luke 6: 13-16 and 9:57-10;20; John 1:35-51; Acts1:5-26 and 2:37-41; Eph. 4:1-7 and 10-16; 3 John: 9-20.

24. **Courtesy/Hospitality**: offering polite and respectful treatment to others as well as treating guests and strangers in a friendly and generous manner.   It also includes receiving the same treatment from others.

Peter 4:7-11.

25. **Creativity/Ideation**: the capacity for original thought and expression that brings new ideas and images into a practical and concrete reality in ways that did not previously exist. The concept of creativity relates to the idea of the indwelling Spirit creating a child with Mary; the creation of the church in Acts; and the expression if individual gifts in each of us.

Ps. 104; Luke 1:26-38, 3:21-22 and4:1; John 14;16, 26; Acts 1 and 2; 1 Thess. 5:3; 1 Cor. 12:1-2.

26. **Criteria/Rationality**: the trained capacity to think logically and reasonably based on a formal body of information. The capacity to exercise reason before emotions. The basis for reason in the Christian tradition is

found in the ten commandments and their application in daily life.

Exodus 18 and 20; Ps. 119; Matt. 22:37-40.

27. **Decision/Initiation**: to feel that it is one's responsibility to begin a creative course of action, or to act on one's conscience without external prompting. In the Christian context this value is key to personal spiritual discernment and to making life-giving choices. To discern God's plans in one's life rather than following other desires is considered a gift.

Deut. 18: 20-21 and 30:15-20; John 1:35-51; Luke 5:1-11; 1 Cor. 12:10; 1 John 4:1; 2 John 7.

28. **Design/Pattern/Order**: awareness of the natural arrangement of things plus the ability to create new arrangements through the initiation of arts, ideas or technology, e.g. architecture.

Gen. 1; Ex. 31:1-11; Eph. 2:9-10.

29. **Detachment/Solitude**: the regular discipline of non-attachment that leads to quality relationships with others and the universal order. Basic to the Christian concept of detachment and contemplation is that God's indwelling presence is available to each individual.

1 John 2:12-17; Luke 12:33-34; John 15-17.

30. **Detachment/Transcendence**: exercising spiritual discipline and detachment (emotional and intellectual distancing from daily concerns) so that one experiences a global and visionary perspective due to one's relationship to the universal order. This is done through a personal relationship to the Divine. Basic to the Chrisitan concept of detachment and contemplation is that God's indwelling presence is available to each individual.

John 15-17.

31. **Dexterity/Coordination**: sufficient harmonious interaction of mental and physical functions to perform basic instrumental skills.

1 Cor. 9:24-27.

32. **Discernment/Communal**: the capacity or skill to enable a group or organization to come to consensus deci-

sions relative to long-term planning through openness, reflection and honest interaction.
2 Thess. 2:13-3:18.

33. **Duty/Obligation:** closely following established customs and regulations out of dedication to one's peers and a sense of responsibility to institutional codes.
2 Chron. 8:14-16; Luke 16:7-10.

34. **Economics/Profit**: accumulation of physical wealth to be secure and respected.
Prov. 14:23. (See also Economics/Success.)

35. **Economics/Success**: to attain favorable and prosperous financial results in business through effective control and efficient management of resources.
Matt: 6:1-4; Luke 12:33-34.

36. **Ecority/Aesthetics**: the capacity, skills and personal, organizational or conceptual influence to enable persons to take authority for the created order of the world and to enhance its beauty and balance through creative technology in ways that have worldwide influence. In Genesis the concept that human beings are to be responsible for the earth develops into the concept that a new order of creation is being born.
Gen. 1:26-30; Is. 2:6-9; Rom. 8:18-23; 2 Cor. 5:17.

37. **Education/Certification**: completing a formally prescribed process of learning and receiving documentation of that process.
Prov. 22:6; Eccl. 8:16-17. (See also Education/ Knowledge/Insight.)

38. **Education/Knowledge/Insight**: the experience of ongoing learning as a means of gaining new facts, truths and principles. One is motivated by the occasional reward of new understanding that is gained intuitively.
Prov. 24:3-7; Eccl. 7:19 and23-25; Luke 2:41-50.

39. **Efficiency/Planning**: thinking about and designing acts and purposes in the best possible and least wasteful manner before implementing them.
1 Cor. 12:12-30; Rom. 12:1-13; Eph. 4:7-16. (See also Service/Vocation; Work/Labor; Corporation/New Order.

40. **Empathy**: reflecting and experiencing another's feelings and state of being through a quality of presence that has the consequence of the person seeing him/herself with more clarity, without any words necessarily having been spoken.
Rom. 12:8-21; Rom. 13:8-10; 1 Cor. 13.

41. **Endurance/Patience**: the ability to bear difficult and painful experiences, situations or persons with calmness, stability and perseverance.
Book of Job; Heb. 10:32-39.

42. **Equality/Liberation**: experiencing oneself as having the same value and rights as all other human beings in such a way that one is set free to be that self and to free others to be themselves. This is the critical consciousness of the value of being human.
Matt. 19:13-15; Acts 4:32-25; Col. 3:10.

43. **Equilibrium**: maintaining a peaceful social environment by averting upsets and avoiding conflicts.
Eph. 2:14; Rom. 14:17; Phil. 4:7; Gal. 5:22.

44. **Equity/Rights**: awareness of the moral and ethical claim of all persons, including oneself, to legal, social and economic equality and fairness plus a personal commitment to defend this claim.
Matt. 19:13-15; Acts 4:32-35; Col. 3:10.

45. **Evaluation/Self System**: appreciating an objective appraisal of oneself and being open to what others reflect about oneself as necessary for self-awareness and personal growth. This value relates to the concept of repentance and personal examination.
Mark 1:4-15; John 4:1-30; Luke 3:1-9; Luke 4; Rom. 5:6-11.

46. **Expressiveness/Freedom/Joy**: to share one's feelings and fantasies so openly and spontaneously that others are free to do the same.
1 Sam. 2:1-10; Luke 1:43-56; Gal. 5:1 and 22-26.

47. **Faith/Risk/Vision**: behavioral commitment to values that are considered life-giving even at risk to one's life. Christ's faith was tested in the desert.
Luke 4:1-13; Matt. 6:25-33; Luke 9:18-21; Rom. 1:8-9;

Gal. 5:1-6; Heb. 12:1-12.

48. **Family/Belonging**: the people and places (such as "home") to whom one feels primary bonds of relationship and acceptance and the place of dwelling of one's parents.
   Gen. 1:27-31; Matt. 1-2; Luke 2:41-52; John 15:12-17. (Use a reference Bible for a careful exploration of these references and their Old Testament antecedents.)

49. **Fantasy/Play**: the experience of personal worth through unrestrained imagination and personal amusement. This value relates to the child in each of us and the ability to fantasize hopeful and playful futures for ourselves and those we love.
   2 Cor. 5:16-19; Mark 10:3-16; Luke 9:47-48.

50. **Food/Warmth/Shelter**: personal concern about having adequate physical nourishment, warmth and comfort and a place of refuge from the elements.
   Ex. 16-17; Ps. 23, 31, 5 and 130; Matt. 6:5-34.

51. **Friendship/Belonging**: to have a group of persons with whom one can share on a day-to-day basis.
   1 Sam 18:1-4; John 15: 12-17; 1 Peter 3:8-12.

52. **Function/Physical**: concern about the ability to perform minimal manipulations of the body to care for oneself and concern about the body's internal systems and their ability to function adequately.
   1 Cor. 9:24-27.

53. **Generosity/Service**: to share one's unique gifts and skills with others as a way of serving humanity without expecting reciprocation.
   Luke 6:36-38 and 10: 29-37; 1 Cor. 12 and 13.

54. **Growth/Expansion**: the ability to enable an organization to develop and grow creatively. This assumes skills in management design, organizational, product and market development at a division or corporate level.
   Matt. 28:16-20; Luke 10:1-20; John 16:5-15.

55. **Health/Healing/Harmony**: soundness of mind and body that flows from meeting one's emotional and physi-

cal needs through self-awareness and preventive discipline. This includes an understanding that commitment to maintaining one's inner rhythm and balance relates to positive feelings and fantasy.

Luke 7:1-17; 8:26-56; 1 Cor. 9:24-27.

56. **Hierarchy/Propriety/Order**: the methodical, harmonious arrangement of persons and things ranked above one another in conformity to established standards of what is good and proper within an organization.

Ex. 18:13-17; Sam. 8 and 9; Luke 20:20-26.

57. **Honor**: high respect for the worth, merit or rank of those in authority, e.g. parents, superiors and national leaders.

Ex. 2:12; Prov. 27:10; Eccl. 7:1.

58. **Human Dignity**: consciousness of the basic right of every human being to have respect and to have his/her basic needs met that will allow him/her the opportunity to develop his/her potential.

Luke: 19:29-37; Matt. 5: 1-10 and 11:28; John 3:16; 1 John 2:1-2; James 2: 1-13.

59. **Human Rights/World Social Order**: committing one's talent, education, training and resources to creating the means for every person in the world to experience his/her basic right to such life-giving resources as food, habitat, employment, health and minimal practical education.

John 4:39-42; Rom. 8:18-34; Rev. 4:21.

60. **Independence**: thinking and acting for oneself in matters of opinion, conduct, etc., without being subject to external constraint or authority. Inherent in this value is the basic human dignity -- the right to be fully oneself. The goal of independence is actually interdependence.

Luke 19:29-37; Matt. 5:1-10 and 11:28; John 3:16; 1 John 2:1-2; James 2:1-13; Rom 12:4-9.

61. **Integration/Wholeness**: the inner capacity to organize the personality (mind and body) into a coordinated, harmonious totality.

Matt. 7:21-17; Rom. 12:1-3.

62. **Interdependence**: seeing and acting on the awareness that personal and inter-institutional cooperation are always preferable to individual decision-making. In the Christian context interdependence is analogous to the concept of the Body of Christ.

Rom. 12:4-9; 1 Cor. 12:4-30.

63. **[Self]Interest/Control**: restraining one's feelings and controlling one's personal interests in order to survive physically in the world.

1 John 2:29-3:4-10; Heb. 10:32-39.

64. **Intimacy**: sharing one's full personhood (thoughts, feelings, fantasies and realities) mutually and freely with the total personhood of another on a regular basis. Intimacy is exemplified by Jesus' love of God and his friends and the supportive relationships he enjoyed.

Luke 7:36-8:3; John 11-12:11; John 14 and 20:11-18.

65. **Intimacy and Solitude as Unitive**: the experience of personal harmony that results from a combination of meditative practice, mutual openness and total acceptance of another person which leads to new levels of meaning and awareness of truth in unity with the universal order and connection with the Divine. The model for the western experience of mysticism and contemplative prayer is anticipated by this value.

John 17; Ps. 42:1-2 and 46; Is. 26:1-19.

66. **Justice/Global Distribution**: commitment to the fact that all persons have equal value but different gifts and abilities to contribute to society, combined with the capacity to elicit inter-institutional and governmental collaboration that will help provide the basic life necessities for the poor or disadvantaged in the world.

John 4:39-42; Rom. 8:18-39; Rev. 4:21.

67. **Justice/Social Order**: taking a course of action that addresses, confronts and helps correct conditions of human oppression in order to actualize the truth that every human being is of equal value.

Prov. 21:3; Micah 6:8; Matt. 5 and 23:23; Rom. 3:5-6.

68. **Knowledge/Discovery/Insight**: the pursuit of truth through patterned investigation. One is motivated by increased intuition and unconsciously-gained un-

derstandings of the wholeness of reality.
Luke 2:41-50; John 3; Eph. 3:14-21.

69. **Law/Guide**: seeing authoritative principles and regulations as a means for creating one's own criteria and moral conscience, and questioning those rules until they are clear and meaningful.
1 John 2:3-11.

70. **Law/Rule**: governing one's conduct, action and procedures by the established legal system or code. Living one's life by the rules.
Ex. 20; Ps. 119; 1 Peter 2:13-25.

71. **Leisure/Freesence**: use of time in a way that requires as much skill and concentration as one's work but that totally detaches one from work so that the spontaneous self is free to emerge in a playful and contagious manner.
Eccl. 3:1-15; John 2:1-12, 13:1-16 and 21.

72. **Life/Self-Actualization**: The inner drive toward experiencing and expressing the totality of one's being through spiritual, psychological, physical and mental exercises which enhance the development of one's maximum potential.
Deut. 30:15-20; Matt. 9:14-17; John 10; Rom. 8:18-27.

73. **Limitation/Acceptance**: giving positive mental assent to the reality that one has boundaries and inabilities. This includes an objective self-awareness of one's strengths and potential as well as weakness and inability. The capacity for self-criticism. This value describes the experience of forgiveness and reconciliation. As such it is also the narrative of Christ's passion -- his dying for our sins.
Matt. 8:21-22, chapters 26 and 27; Luke 15:11-32 and 23:33-34; Rom. 3:21-26 and 5-8; Col. 1:19-21; Eph. 2:11-22; Mark 14-15; Luke 22 and 23; 1 Cor. 1:16-21 and 11:17-34.

74. **Limitation/Celebration**: the recognition that one's limits are the framework for exercising one's talents. The ability to laugh at one's own imperfections. Christ defeated our limitations, even the limitation of death and rose again. This is the value of personal growth

and resurrection. It is expressed ritually through the act of communion or remembering the Lord's Supper.
Matt. 28; Mark 16; Luke 24; John 20 and 21; Acts 1:1-11; Rom. 5-8; 1 Cor. 10:16-21 and 11:17-34.

75. **Loyalty/Fidelity**: strict observance of promises and duties to those in authority and to those in close personal relationships.
Prov. 66:1-6; Eccl. 10:1-11; Luke 22:54-62; John 21; Rom. 3:20-31.

76. **Macroeconomics/World Order**: the ability to manage and direct the use of financial resources at an institutional and inter-institutional level toward creating a more stable and equitable world economic order. This value is recent in history. As such Scripture only guides the attitudes we have toward the right use of global financial resources.
Matt. 6:1-4; Luke 12:33-34; Rev. 21:1-2. (See also Construction/New Order.)

77. **Management**: the control and direction of personnel in a business or institution for the purpose of optimal productivity and efficiency. In Latin "ad" means "to" therefore management as administration means "to minister to."
1 Cor. 12:12-30; Rom. 12:1-13; Eph. 4:7-16. (See also Service/Vocation; Work/Labor; Corporation/New Order.

78. **Memberships/Institution**: the pride of belonging to and functioning as an integral part of an organization, foundation, establishment, etc.
Matt. 4:18-22, 10:1-42 and 16:13-20; Acts 1:12-2:47.

79. **Minessence**: the capacity to miniaturize and simplify complex ideas or technological instruments (tools) into concrete and practical objectifications in a way that creatively alters the consciousness of the user. Minessence is related to the power of the Holy Spirit within. The pre-eminent examples of this value are the creation and the coming of Christ.
Gen. 1: Ps. 104; Ezek. 36:27-37:14; Luke 1:26-38 and 3:21-22; John 1:1-14, 14:16 and 26; Acts 1 and 2; 1Thess. 5:23; 1 Cor. 12:1-11.

80. **Mission/Objectives**: the ability to establish organization-al goals and execute long-term planning that takes into consideration the needs of society and the way the organization contributes to those needs.
Matt. 28:16-20; Luke 10:1-20; John 16:5-15.

81. **Mutual Responsibility/Accountability**: the skills to main-tain a reciprocal balance of tasks and assignments with others so that everyone is answerable for his/her own area of responsibility. This requires the abili-ty to mobilize one's anger in creative and supportive ways so as to move relationships to increasing levels of cooperation.
Matt. 5 - 7, especially 5:1-12 and 19:19; Ex. 20:12-16; Deut. 5:16-20. (See also Law/Rule; Law/Guide; Duty/Obligation; Responsibility; Obedience/Duty; Obedience/ Mutual Accountability.)

82. **Obedience/Duty**: dutifully and submissively complying with moral and legal obligations established by par-ents and civic and religious authorities.
Phil. 2:5-13.

83. **Obedience/Mutual Accountability**: being mutually and equally responsible for establishing and being sub-ject to a common set of rules and guidelines in a group of persons.
1 Cor. 12:12-30; Col. 2:9-10.

84. **Ownership**: personal and legal possession of skills, deci-sions, and property that gives one a sense of personal authority. In the Christian context skills are consid-ered "gifts."
Acts 2:38-40; 1 Cor. 12:4-11, 27-31; 1 Tim. 2:1-7; 2 Tim. 2:15.

85. **Patriotism/Esteem**: honor for one's country based on per-sonal devotion, love and support.
Rom. 13:1-10.

86. **Personal/Authority/Honesty**: the freedom to experience and express one's full range of feelings and thoughts in a straightforward, objective manner. This ability comes from a personal integration of thoughts and feelings and results in experiencing one's own integri-ty and power.

Eccl. 1:16-2:14; Matt 18:1-18; Luke 20.

87. **Physical Delight**: the joy of experiencing all the senses of one's body. In the Christian context the body is valued in its own right as a sacred temple and as part of God's valued creation.
Luke 1:26-38; John 11:1-12:19; Rom. 8 and 15:35-58.

88. **Pioneerism/Innovation/Progress**: introducing and originating creative ideas for positive change in social organizations and systems and providing the framework for actualizing them.
Acts 1 and 2; 1 Thess. 5:23; 1 Cor. 12:1-11; Rom. 12:4-9; 1 Cor. 12:4-30.

89. **Play/Recreation**: a pastime or diversion from the anxiety of day-to-day living for the purpose of undirected, spontaneous refreshment (which provides for a potential self to be experienced).
Ex. 2:9-10; John 2:1-12.

90. **Presence/Dwelling**: the ability to be with another person that comes from inner self-knowledge which is so contagious that another person is able to ponder the depths of who he or she is with awareness and clarity.
Ex. 3:1-15 and 24:16; John 1:14, 12:1-8 and 21.

91. **[Self]Preservation**: doing what is necessary to protect oneself from physical harm or destruction in an alien world.
Ps. 23, 31, 55 and 130; Matt 6:25-34.

92. **Prestige/Image**: physical appearance which reflects success and achievement, gains the esteem of others and promotes success.
2 Chron. 20:20-21; Job 36 and 42; Eccl. 8; Jas. 1:22-25.

93. **Productivity**: to feel energized by generating and completing tasks and activities and achieving externally established goals and expectations.
Job 36 and 42; Eccl. 7:13;11

94. **Property/Control**: accumulating property and exercising personal direction over it for security and for meeting one's basic physical and emotional needs.
Luke 16:1-13 and 19-31.

95. **Prophet/Vision**: the ability to communicate the truth about global justice issues and human rights in such a lucid manner that the hearers are able to transcend their limited personal awareness and gain a new perspective on themselves and the needs of others.

   The Old Testament is full of works of prophets. The pre-eminent model is Moses. For Christians the model is Jesus of Nazareth who calls us to follow him. Jesus examined his own role as prophet in the desert. We are to be as Jesus was.

   Ex.; John 12:41-45 and 15-17; Matt. 4:1-16; Luke 4:1-14 and 9:1-6; 1 Cor. 12:4-11.

96. **Relaxation**: diversion from physical or mental work which reduces stress and provides a balance of work and play as a means of realizing one's potential.

   John 2:1-12. (See also Play/Recreation; Leisure/ Freesence.)

97. **Research/Originality/Knowledge**: systematic investigation and contemplation of the nature of truths and principles about people and human experience for the purpose of creating new insights and awareness.

   The concept of creativity relates to the idea of the Holy Spirit within creating a child with Mary, the creation of The Church and the expression of individual gifts in each of us.

   Ezek. 36:27-37:14; Luke 1:26-38, 3:21-22 and 4:1; John 14:16, 26; Acts 1 and 2; 1 Thess. 5:23; 1 Cor. 12:1-11.

98. **Responsibility**: to be personally accountable for and in charge of a specific area or course of action in one's organization or group. The concept of creativity relates to the idea of the indwelling spirit.

   Ezek. 18. (See also Mutual Responsibility/Accountability.)

99. **Rights/Respect**: the moral principle of esteeming the worth (and property) of another as I expect others to esteem me (and mine).

   Prov. 21:2-6; Col. 3:8-10. (See also [Self] Worth; Equity/Rights.)

100. **Ritual/Communication**: skills and use of liturgy and the arts as a communication medium for raising critical

consciousness of such themes as world social conditions and awareness of the transcendent.
Ex. 30:30-35; 1 Cor. 10:16-21 and 11:17-34.

101. **Rule/Accountability**: the need to have each person openly explain or justify his/her behavior in relationship to the established codes of conduct, procedures, etc.
Ex. 20; Ps. 119; 1 Peter 2:13-25.

102. **Safety/Survival**: concern about the ability to avoid personal injury, danger or loss and to do what is necessary to protect oneself in adverse circumstances.
Ps. 23, 25, 55 and 130; Matt. 6:25-34.

103. **Search/Meaning/Hope**: a personal exploration arising from an inner longing and curiosity to integrate one's feelings, imagination and objective knowledge in order to discover one's unique place in the world.
Luke 11:9-13; Rom. 8:24-27.

104. **Security**: finding a safe place or relationship where one experiences protection and is free from cares and anxieties.
Ps. 23 and 91; Prov. 14:26; Matt. 6:25-34.

105. **Sensory Pleasure/Sexuality**: gratifying one's sensual desires and experiencing one's sexual identity. In the Christian context the body is a holy vessel of God's creation. The value applies to the way we treat ourselves and others.
Rom. 12:1-2; 1 Cor. 6:12-20; Eph. 5:28-33.

106. **Service/Vocation**: to be motivated to use one's unique gifts and skills to contribute to society through one's occupation, business, profession or calling.
Matt. 5:1-4; 1 Cor. 12 and 13; Gal. 5:13-26.

107. **Sharing/Listening/Trust**: the capacity to actively and accurately hear another's thoughts and feelings and to express one's own thoughts and feelings in a climate of mutual confidence in each other's integrity.
Ps. 56; John 17.

108. **Simplicity/Play**: the capacity for deeply appreciating the world combined with a playful attitude toward organizations and systems that is energizing and positive.

The ability to see simplicity in complexity and to be detached from the world as primarily material in nature.
Luke 9:57-62, 12:22-32 and 14:7-35; John 16 and 17.

109. **Social Affirmation**: personal respect and validation coming from the support and respect of one's peers which is necessary for one to grow and succeed.
Prov. 21:2-6; Col. 3:8-10; John 1:1-14. (See also [Self] Worth; Being Liked; Friendship/Belonging.

110. **Support/Peer**: to have persons who are one's equals and who sustain one in both joyful and difficult times.
John 15:12-17; 1 Peter 3:8-12.

111. **Synergy**: experiencing the relationships of persons within a group to be harmonious and energized so that the outcome of the group far surpasses its predicted ability based on the total abilities of its individual members.

The concept of synergy is an integral part of the creative process. In the Christian context creativity relates to the concept of the indwelling Spirit creating a child with Mary, the creation of the Church and the expression of individual gifts.
Ps. 104; Ezek. 36:27-37:14; Luke 1:26-38, 3:21-22 and 4:1; John 14:16; Acts 1 and 2; 1 Thess. 5:23; 1 Cor. 12:1-11.

112. **Technology/Science**: systematic knowledge of the physical or natural world and practical applications of the knowledge through person-made devices and tools. In the Christian context our attitudes about science are rooted in our place in the creation. And, the goals of science are always within the appropriate framework of love.
Gen. 1:26-31; Job 38 and 39; Eph. 2:9-10; 1 Cor. 13;1-3.

113. **Territory/Security**: provision for physically defending property, a personal domain or nation state.
Exodus; Joshua; Samuel; Kings.

114. **Tradition**: recognizing the importance of ritualizing family history, religious history and national history in one's life so as to enrich its meaning. The first five

books of the Bible and the four Gospels form the basis of Christian tradition.
Ps. 105; Luke 1.

115. **Transcendence/Global Equality**: knowing the practical relationship between human oppression, freedom and creative ecological balance based on a simultaneous awareness of the finite and the infinite so that one can influence changes that promote greater human equality.
Luke 1:46-55; Rev. 21 and 22.

116. **Truth/Wisdom/Integrated Insight**: intense pursuit and discovery of ultimate truth above all other activities. This results in intimate knowledge of objective and subjective realities which converge into the capacity to clearly comprehend persons and systems and their interrelationship.
Prov. 8 and 9; John 3:19-21 and 8:12; 1 John 1:5-7.

117. **Unity/Diversity**: recognizing and acting administratively on the belief that an organization is creatively enhanced by giving equal opportunity to persons from a variety of cultures, ethnic backgrounds and diverse training. In the Christian context this is analogous to the Body of Christ.
Rom. 12:4-9; 1 Cor. 12:4-30.

118. **Unity/Uniformity**: harmony and agreement in an institution that is established to achieve efficiency, order, loyalty and conformity to established norms.

Ex. 18:13-27; 1 Sam. 8 and 9; Luke 20:20-26.

119. **Wonder/Awe/Fate**: to be filled with marvel, amazement and fear when faced with the overwhelming grandeur and power of one's physical environment.
Gen. 1; Ps. 24 and 121; Job 35.

120. **Wonder/Curiosity/Nature**: a sense of marvel and amazement about the physical world coupled with a desire to learn about it and explore it personally.
Gen. 1; Ps. 24 and 121; Job 38 and 39.

121. **Word**: the ability to communicate universal truths so effectively that the hearer becomes conscious of his/her limitations such that life and hope are renewed in

the individual hearer.

Gen. 1; John 1:1-14 and 15; Acts 2:1-13; 1 John 1:1-4.

122. **Work/Labor**: to have skills and rights that allow one to produce a minimal living for oneself and one's family.

Ex. 34:21; Gen. 26:12; John 5:17 and 6:27; Luke 10:1-2.

123. **Workmanship/Art/Craft**: skills requiring manual dexterity that produce artifacts and modify or beautify the person-made environment. In the Bible skilled craftspeople were always held in the highest esteem.

Ex. 3:1-11; Acts 18:3; Eph. 2:9-10.

124. **Worship/Faith/Creed**: reverence for and belief in God, that is expressed and experienced through a commitment to doctrines and teachings of religious belief. Worship gives "worth" or meaning to God as expressed so clearly in the Psalms.

Ps. 146-150; Ex. 30:30-35; John 4:20-24.

125. **[Self]Worth**: the knowledge that when those one respects and esteems really know him/her, they will affirm that he/she is worthy of that respect. God loves and esteems us so much that Jesus became human in order to save us. For the Christian self- worth means accepting the Incarnation of Jesus Christ as a model for what it means to be fully human.

John 1:8-25, 3:16 and 10:29-31; Luke 1:25-56; Rom. 5.